Whispers
Of
The
Soul

Copyright © 2025 by Kelvin Cook

All rights reserved.

No part of this publication may be reproduced, distributed, or transmitted in any form or by any means, including photocopying, recording, or other electronic or mechanical methods, without the prior written permission of the publisher, except as permitted by U.S. copyright law.

ISBN: 979-8-9991603-1-7

THE HOLY BIBLE, NEW INTERNATIONAL VERSION®, NIV® Copyright © 1973, 1978, 1984, 2011 by Biblica, Inc.® Used by permission. All rights reserved worldwide.
Some Scriptures are quoted from the King James Version, KJV

Publisher: Greater Is Required, LLC Publishing Services

Introduction:	9
Personal Note:	10
Author Bio:	11
Preface:	12
Section I: Sacred Longing (The Call Within)	13
First Love	14
The Light to My Darkness	15
A King's Love for His Queen	16
Unbreakable Bond	17
The 5 Senses of Love	18
Falling in Love, Dying Without It	19
A Man's Love for a Woman He Can Never Deserve	20
A Love That Burns Like Fire	21
Love's Fragile Thread	22
Our Souls Intertwined	23
Section II: The Touch of Memory (Honoring the Past)	24
Where the Pain Lives	25
The Weight I Carry	26
I Am Still Here	27
The Mirror Lied	28
When Grief Speaks	29
The Silence Between Us	30
The Child I Buried Inside Me	31
The Bruises No One Sees	32
A Cage with No Locks	33
The Art of Letting Go	34
Section III: The Garden of Becoming (Growth & Transformation)	35
Finding Myself	36
The Journey Within	37

Unchained Spirit	38
Healing from the Hurt	39
The Mirror Tells No Lies	40
The Power of Self-Worth	41
One Foot In, One Foot Out	42
Escaping the Shadows	43
Survival vs. Love	44
A Letter to My Past Self	45
Section IV: The Weight of Love (Heartbreak & Healing)	**46**
Echoes of a Fading Soul	47
Living & Leaving	48
A Conversation with Death	49
Regret: The Last Breath	50
Dying Young, Dying Old	51
The Cost of Time	52
Goodbye	53
What We Take for Granted	54
Living to Impress, Dying Unfulfilled	55
The Final Whisper	56
Section V: Devotion and Depth (Spiritual Intimacy)	**57**
A Father's Promise	58
Roots That Run Deep	59
The Strength of a Name	60
Grandma's Unbreakable Love	61
A Mother's Pain	62
The Weight of a Father's Shoulders	63
Lessons Passed Down	64
For the Ones Who Raised Me	65
The Unseen Sacrifices	66
Family: The Blood That Binds Us	67
Section VI: The Voice Within (Identity & Empowerment)	**68**
A Black Man's Burden	69

The Streets Keep Calling	70
The Cost of Survival	71
Gun Violence in Milwaukee	72
The Forgotten Souls of Our City	73
The Price of Being a Black Man	74
Police Brutality: A Stolen Breath	75
The Weight of the World on Our Shoulders	76
Black Men, We Must Do Better	77
The Revolution Within	78
Section VII: Divine Whispers (Faith & Spirituality)	**79**
When God Found Me	80
Whispers in the Stillness	81
Faith That Walks Through Fire	82
I Am Not Alone	83
A Prayer for the Wounded	84
God of the Second Chance	85
Strength in Surrender	86
My Heart Belongs to God	87
Built by Grace	88
Whispers of the Soul	89
Reflections & Scriptures	**90**
Section I: Echoes of the Heart	**90**
Section II: Scars & Shadows	**91**
Section III: Roads to Redemption	**92**
Section IV: Life's Fragile Dance	**93**
Section V: Seeds of the Soul	**94**
Section VI: Fire & Fury	**95**
Section VII: Divine Whispers	**96**
Reader's Prayer	**97**
Section I: The Cry Beneath the Silence	**99**
The Cry I Never Spoke	100
Tears Behind the Eyes	101

The Silence Between My Prayers	102
What My Smile Doesn't Say	103
The Weight I Carry in Secret	105
The Ache That Has No Name	107
When I Couldn't Say Help	108
Smiling Through Survival	109
Numb	110
The Healing in Being Heard	111
Section II: Shattered Mirrors	**112**
The Mirror Lied to Me	113
The Me I Hide from Myself	114
Cracked but Still Crowned	115
What Shame Left Behind	116
Reflections from a Wounded Soul	117
The Pieces They Never See	118
When I Believed I Wasn't Enough	119
The Lie of Perfection	120
The Mask I Forgot to Take Off	121
Through the Cracks, I Saw God	122
Section III: Dust and Water	**123**
Clay in the Potter's Hands	124
We Were Made of Dust and Glory	125
Baptized by My Own Tears	126
When Water Found My Wounds	127
Fragile but Full of Faith	128
Lessons from the River	129
The Softening	130
Stillness in the Storm	131
The Water Remembers Me	132
Where Dust Meets Grace	133
Section IV: Songs of the Womb	**134**
Before You Had a Name	135

The First Song Was a Mother's Cry	136
My Body Was a Garden	137
A Father's Voice in the Dark	138
Carried in More Than My Womb	139
The Man I Had to Become	140
The Secret Weight of Motherhood	141
To My Child I Haven't Met Yet	142
Fatherhood Is Forgiveness	143
Songs of the Womb	144
Section V: Midnight Conversations	**145**
When the World Goes Quiet	146
Prayers with No Language	147
Conversations I Never Had	148
The Clock Doesn't Care	149
Nights I Sleep Next to My Fears	150
A Letter to My Future Self	151
When Love Doesn't Come Back	152
The Things I Can't Tell Them	153
Midnight Is When I Remember	154
Conversations with God at 3AM	155
Section VI: The Weight of Mercy	**156**
The Weight of Mercy	157
Grace Wore My Scars	158
Mercy Met Me in the Mud	159
The Man I Used to Be	160
The Guilt That Tried to Own Me	161
I Don't Deserve This Kind of Love	162
When Forgiveness Found Me	163
Ashes and Altars	164
The Quiet After Repentance	165
I Am Not Who I Was	166
Section VII: When the Spirit Sings	**167**

When the Spirit Sings	168
Breath of the Divine	169
Heaven Touched Earth in Me	170
Surrender in the Silence	171
My Spirit Remembers	172
The Holy That Lives in Me	173
Spirit Over Flesh	174
The Sound of Deliverance	175
I Am His Vessel	176
When the Spirit Sings	177
Section I: Beneath the Silence	**178**
Section II: Shattered Mirrors	**178**
Section III: Dust and Water	**179**
Section IV: Songs of the Womb	**179**
Section V: Midnight Conversations	**180**
Section VI: The Weight of Mercy	**180**
Section VII: When the Spirit Sings	**181**
Final Benediction	**182**

Introduction:

Whispers of the Soul is not merely a collection of poems — it is a quiet unfolding of everything I've ever held close to the heart. These pages carry the weight of love gained and lost, the ache of grief, the resilience born through struggle, and the still, sacred moments when God speaks through silence.

This book was written from a place of truth. A place where vulnerability meets strength, where brokenness becomes beauty, and where pain dares to become poetry. Every line you read has lived somewhere — in my past, my present, my prayers, or in the shadows of what I've overcome.

You'll find in these chapters' stories of passion and heartbreak, of mental battles fought in silence, of family, of legacy, of spiritual awakening, and of conversations I've only ever had with God. Some verses may feel like they were written for you because in a way, they were. Whether you are healing, growing, weeping, or believing again... there is room for you here.

Let this book be your mirror, your companion, and your reminder that you are not alone. That you have a soul worth listening to — and it still whispers truth even in your darkest hours.

So take a deep breath, turn the page, and walk with me.

This is the sound of healing.

This is Whispers of the Soul.

The LORD is close to the brokenhearted and saves those who are crushed in spirit."

— Psalm 34:18 (NIV

Personal Note:

Every word in this book carries a piece of me, my journey, my pain, my love, my reflections on the world around me. Whispers of the Soul is more than a collection of poems; it is a window into the depths of my heart, a conversation with the unseen, a voice for emotions too heavy to speak aloud.

I have lived, loved, lost, and searched for meaning in places both light and dark. Poetry has **been** my sanctuary, my way of making sense of the chaos, of finding beauty even in brokenness. Every poem within these pages was born from real moments—some joyful, some heartbreaking, all deeply human.

This book is for those who have ever felt unheard, unseen, or misunderstood. For the ones who carry wounds in silence, for those who have battled with love, identity, pain, and the longing for something greater. I want these words to sit with you in your quietest moments, to remind you that you are not alone, that your emotions are valid, and that even the darkest nights hold whispers of light.

To those who have inspired me—whether through love, lessons, or loss—this book is my gratitude. And to you, the reader, I hope you find pieces of yourself within these pages. Let these words be a companion, a mirror, and a reminder that no matter where you are on your journey, your soul still speaks, and it is worth listening to

Author Bio:

Kelvin Cook is a passionate writer, entrepreneur, and spiritual seeker whose work bridges the emotional with the eternal. A poet by purpose, Kelvin is a devoted father working toward building generational wealth and emotional healing through art, service, and faith.

His debut poetry series, Whispers of the Soul, invites readers into the depths of love, loss, redemption, and divine reflection. With raw honesty and soulful intention, Kelvin's words speak not only to the wounds we carry but to the healing we're all worthy of.

He currently resides in Milwaukee, Wisconsin, where he continues to write, build, and inspire others to find meaning in both the struggle and the light.

Preface:

Poetry has a way of reaching into the deepest corners of the heart, pulling out emotions we often struggle to name. Whispers of the Soul is not just a collection of words, it is a journey through love and loss, pain and healing, self-discovery and redemption. These poems are the echoes of experiences, both personal and universal, woven into verses that speak to the human condition.

This book is for those who have felt unseen, for the lovers and the lost, for the dreamers and the broken. Every line is a whisper, a message from the soul, urging you to feel, to reflect, and to remember that even in darkness, there is light.

Through these pages, you may find pieces of yourself, your past, your present, or the person you are striving to become. May these words touch your heart, stir your spirit, and remind you that your story is still being written

"Where the heart bleeds, the soul speaks. And when the soul whispers—healing begins."

—K.C.

Psalm 42:7 (NIV)

"Deep calls to deep in the roar of your waterfalls; all your waves and breakers have swept over me."

Section I: Sacred Longing (The Call Within)

This section captures the inner ache of the soul—our longing for purpose, peace, healing, and connection. It's about the quiet pull we feel in our spirit, a divine invitation to seek more: more meaning, more love, more of God.

Scriptures:

Psalm 42:1-2 (NIV) "As the deer pants for streams of water, so my soul pants for you, my God. My soul thirsts for God, for the living God."

Matthew 5:6 (NIV) "Blessed are those who hunger and thirst for righteousness, for they will be filled."

Ecclesiastes 3:11 (NIV) "He has made everything beautiful in its time. He has also set eternity in the human heart; yet no one can fathom what God has done from beginning to end.

First Love

I remember you like a melody too soft for the world to hold
a whisper of wonder that wrapped itself around my ribs
and taught my young heart how to sing.
Before heartbreak, before fear, before I knew what it meant to lose,
there was you smiling in a light I thought would never dim,
touching my hand like I was something sacred. We were clumsy,
like two souls learning to dance in the dark,
but in those moments, we believed in forever
as if it was stitched into the sky just for us.
You wrote your name on my spirit with laughter,
with butterflies fluttering where logic should have been,
and I let you in without hesitation, without walls, without questions.
There was no roadmap, no rules, no reason, just your eyes and mine,
meeting in a thousand unspoken promises.
And though time moved on, and life untangled our bond,
you remain—the echo of innocence,
the first spark that ignited my understanding of love.
You taught me that love is both a gift and a gamble,
and even though we didn't last, you left me fuller,
softer, braver. First love isn't meant to be perfect
only unforgettable. And you are.

The Light to My Darkness

When the world wrapped me in silence,
and shadows tucked themselves into my chest,
you appeared not as a savior,
but as a soul who saw the storm inside me
and chose to sit beside it. You didn't demand the sun
you became it.
You didn't try to fix what broke inside of me,
you held the pieces
like they were something beautiful.
In a world where people fear the dark, you saw mine
and said, "I'm not afraid."
Your love, patient and warm,
slowly stitched light into the cracks I had forgotten.
You didn't rush the healing. You whispered hope
into the places I buried it. And I?
I grew in your warmth.
Like morning reaching through shattered windows,
I rose, not perfect but present. Still hurting— but whole.
You are not my escape. You are the reason I stay.
In my darkest nights, you didn't run.
You lit a candle and waited with me
until I could finally see myself again.

A King's Love for His Queen

I don't just love you.
I honor you. In a world that's forgotten what royalty feels like,
I see your crown—even when it's heavy,
even when the world tries to knock it off.
You are my balance, my fire, the soft to my strength,
and the strength when I fall short.
My love for you isn't performance— it's purpose.
To protect your peace, to uplift your dreams,
to whisper to your doubts, "You are more than enough."
I see the battles you fight in silence,
the grace you carry like armor.
You deserve more than flowers and poems
you deserve loyalty that does not waver,
even when tested by the winds of life.
I vow to lead not with ego, but with empathy,
to listen when you're tired,
to hold you when your world feels too loud,
and to remind you that
A true king serves his queen with reverence.
For in loving you, I am elevated.
And in you loving me,
I find peace.

Unbreakable Bond

They called us foolish.

Said we'd never last.

But they didn't see

how your laugh stitched light into my chest,

how your tears felt like mine,

how your silence spoke louder than any words.

We don't always agree.

Sometimes we break.

But never apart.

This love isn't fragile.

It's weathered, worn, tested by time

yet still standing.

It's built on forgiveness,

on sleepless nights and early mornings,

on prayers whispered into pillows, and apologies wrapped in kisses.

You are not just my partner. You are my mirror.

The one who sees the worst in me

and still chooses the best.

We may bend, but we never break.

Because what we've built isn't just a love story

it's a legacy of choosing each other

every damn time.

The 5 Senses of Love

I see you

not just your beauty, but your soul glowing behind tired eyes,

the way your joy softens a room, and your pain sharpens it.

I hear you

in the silence between words, in the heartbeat beneath your laughter,

in the way you say my name

like a song only you could write.

I taste love

in the mornings you kiss me before coffee,

in the sweetness of your forgiveness,

in every tear that finds its way to my lips

when we're too human to be perfect but still refuse to let go.

I smell you

in memories, in t-shirts, in air thick with longing.

The scent of home, not a place, but a presence

that lingers long after you leave.

I feel you

in the warmth of your hand, the chill when you're gone,

the pulse beneath my ribs

reminding me that love

isn't just something I fall into

it's something I live through.

Falling in Love, Dying Without It

To love you was to learn how to fly

without wings

to leap into the unknown

and find your arms waiting like sky. Every glance, a sunrise.

Every touch, resurrection.

But now that you're gone, the air feels heavier.

I breathe, but I don't live.

I exist in echoes

of what used to be laughter, used to be warmth.

Falling in love was the most beautiful ache

a free fall into something divine.

But now I walk with gravity

pulling harder than before,

each day a quiet death

without your voice in it.

And yet, I would do it again

choose the fall,

knowing the crash.

Because loving you

was worth every piece it broke.

Some loves don't last.

But they never leave.

A Man's Love for a Woman He Can Never Deserve

I watch you love me

with a grace I never earned,

a patience I don't deserve,

and I wonder what you see in a man

still trying to unlearn his demons.

You hold my flaws like fragile glass,

never trying to fix them,

just loving them enough

that they don't feel sharp anymore.

I want to be better for you.

But some days, I am the storm

and you are the roof

that refuses to break.

I ache knowing you could have chosen easier,

someone polished, someone whole.

But you chose me

and in doing so, you teach me to choose myself.

I may never deserve your kind of love,

but I will spend every day

trying to rise to it.

A Love That Burns Like Fire

We don't love quietly.

We crash.

We blaze.

We burn.

Your kiss is gasoline.

My words are sparks.

Every glance between us

is a wildfire waiting to erupt.

We argue like thunder.

We make up like rain.

Ours is not a calm river

it's an ocean storm, pulling us under

just to remind us how deep this goes.

But even in the chaos, I never doubt.

Because beneath the fire

is a foundation unshaken.

You are my burn,

and my balm.

Some love stories are soft.

Ours is scorched into the stars

dangerous, beautiful,

eternal.

Love's Fragile Thread

We hold each other like glass

beautiful, breakable, full of light but trembling in our palms.

Love isn't always loud.

Sometimes it's a whisper

barely hanging on

through long nights and heavy silences.

One thread.

That's all we have sometimes. A single promise

stretched between two weary souls

who refuse to let go. There are days we want to.

When words fail. When wounds speak louder than our hearts.

But we stay. And that is the miracle.

Love is not always passion.

Sometimes it's persistence.

It's reaching across the void

with trembling fingers

saying, "I still choose you. Even when it hurts.

Even when it's hard. Even when it's easier not to.

We are stitched together

by something fragile

but it holds.

And it always will.

Our Souls Intertwined

I don't just love you.

I remember you

from before this life,

from dreams I had before I could speak.

We meet in a place words can't reach.

Our connection isn't chance

it's soul-deep, ancient, etched into time's very fabric.

When I look at you, it's not your face I recognize

it's your spirit.

It calls mine like a song

only we know.

No matter the distance,

no matter the storms, we find our way back

again and again.

Lifetimes couldn't break what we are.

Because this love?

It's written in the stars. Not borrowed.

Not forced. Just true.

Our souls are not two, but one stretched across this life

and the next.

And in you,

I finally found home.

Section II: The Touch of Memory (Honoring the Past)

This section is a reflection on the people, moments, and seasons that shaped us. It honors both joy and pain, cherishing where we've come from while allowing space for healing and gratitude.

Scriptures:

Deuteronomy 6:12 (NIV) "Be careful that you do not forget the Lord, who brought you out of Egypt, out of the land of slavery."

Isaiah 46:9 (NIV) "Remember the former things, those of long ago; I am God, and there is no other..."

Psalm 77:11 (NIV) "I will remember the deeds of the Lord; yes, I will remember your miracles of long ago."

Where the Pain Lives

There's a place in me I rarely let others see.

A corner dimly lit, where echoes of old heartbreak still whisper,

where betrayal wears familiar faces

and forgiveness has yet to bloom.

I smile on the outside.

I laugh. I carry on. But inside

there's a house with no windows,

just walls built from the things I never said,

and doors that won't open

because I've nailed them shut with fear.

I wish healing was a straight line.

But it's not. It's jagged and uneven,

filled with nights where the silence screams

louder than anything else.

Still, I return to this place not to dwell,

but to dust the floor, to hang pictures of progress,

to make peace with the ghost

of who I used to be.

Because I can't heal

what I pretend doesn't hurt.

And I can't grow if I don't know where the pain lives.

The Weight I Carry

I carry things I can't name.

Not in my hands—

but in my spirit, in the slow ache of waking up,

in the way my smile sometimes trembles

at the corners.

There are memories that never left.

Words I swallowed

because the world said "be strong." Tears I hid

because I didn't want to burden anyone else.

But strength isn't silence. It's surviving

when everything in you says "give up."

It's carrying the weight

without letting it crush the goodness still in you.

Some days I want to set it all down

the regrets, the grief,

the versions of me that didn't make it.

But even if I can't yet let them go,

I can shift them. Rearrange them.

Make them lighter with every deep breath.

I may carry pain— but I also carry grace.

And grace knows how to hold it all

without breaking.

I Am Still Here

They tried to break me.

Life, Loss, Loneliness.

But look—

I am still here.

I've bled in silence.

I've shattered without sound.

I've smiled when my soul

was begging for someone to notice the cracks.

But I didn't vanish. I didn't give up.

Even when every part of me

screamed for rest that couldn't be found,

I kept breathing.

This heart?

It has been through war.

And yet, it still beats

like it believes in something better.

So let the world see the scars.

They are not shame— they are survival.

They are proof that no matter what tried to bury me,

I rose.

I am still here.

And that matters more than perfection ever could.

The Mirror Lied

The mirror said I was broken.

It pointed at my flaws, highlighted every scar,

made music of my missteps.

I believed it for years.

Thought I had to be prettier, stronger, more healed, less human.

But mirrors don't show soul.

They don't reflect kindness, or compassion,

or the courage it takes

to get up after life has knocked you down.

I've come to understand

the reflection is just a shell.

The truth lives beneath the skin

in the battles I've won quietly,

in the love I give freely,

in the way I keep going

when nothing makes sense.

So now, when I look in the mirror,

I see more than flaws. I see a survivor.

A healer. A heart that still beats

despite everything.

The mirror lied. But my spirit?

It never did.

When Grief Speaks

Grief doesn't knock.

It barges in

uninvited, unapologetic.

One moment you're laughing,

the next you're drowning

in memories that feel too heavy to carry.

It wears a thousand faces.

A song, A scent.

An empty seat at the table.

And it doesn't get smaller.

You just grow around it.

There is no fixing it.

No magic to erase it.

Only space to feel it

Fully, Raw, Real.

Sometimes I talk to the ones I've lost,

not because I expect an answer,

but because love doesn't disappear

just because a heartbeat did.

Grief isn't weakness.

It's a sign that we loved deeply.

And love that deep? Never dies.

The Silence Between Us

We used to speak without words.

Now we sit in a silence

that feels louder than anything we've ever said.

It isn't anger that keeps us apart—

it's the weight of everything unspoken,

piling up like ash after a fire

that neither of us knew how to control.

I reach for you in my mind

more than I reach with my hands.

Because I'm not sure

if your touch would heal me

or hurt me more.

And still— I miss you.

The you I knew before pain rewrote our story,

before we learned

that even love can't always fix

what's already fractured.

If silence had a voice,

it would echo with everything

we never had the courage to say:

"I'm sorry. "I'm hurting too."

"I still care, but I don't know how to stay."

The Child I Buried Inside Me

There was once a child inside me

wild-eyed, fearless,

hopeful beyond reason.

He danced in the light of dreams,

spoke his truth without apology,

and loved without a single wall.

But life... Life taught him to be quiet.

To hide. To flinch at kindness

because it often came with pain.

Piece by piece, I buried him.

Under expectations.

Under heartbreak.

Under the belief

that innocence is weakness

and vulnerability is a wound waiting to be reopened.

Now, I dig.

Slowly, Carefully.

Through layers of shame and silence,

to find him again.

Because healing isn't just about surviving.

It's about remembering who I was

before the world told me who I had to be.

The Bruises No One Sees

Not all wounds bleed.

Not all pain screams.

Some of it hides beneath perfectly timed smiles

and practiced responses:

"I'm fine." "I'm okay." "I'm just tired."

But I've been tired for longer than I can admit.

Tired of carrying what no one else can see.

Tired of pretending that I don't feel hollow on the inside.

There are bruises that never show on the soul, on the heart,

in the mind that replays past failures

like a broken record.

And still, I wake up.

Still, I push forward.

Still, I try to believe

that one day,

these invisible bruises

will become the very places

my light shines through.

Because pain is real but so is healing.

And maybe—just maybe—

the beauty is in being able to walk wounded,

And still choose love.

A Cage with No Locks

I built a cage

to keep myself safe.

Forged from past hurts,

from betrayals that cut too deep,

from nights I cried alone

and mornings I rose pretending I didn't.

It had no locks, no keys, no captor.

Just me— trapped in the memory of who I was

when I got hurt.

I convinced myself it was better this way.

No risks. No love. No pain.

But also— no joy.

No connection. No freedom.

Then one day, I looked closer.

Realized the door was always open.

And the only thing keeping me inside

was fear of feeling again.

So I stepped out.

Shaking. But free.

Not because the pain was gone,

but because I finally chose to live anyway.

The Art of Letting Go

Letting go is not forgetting.

It's not pretending it never mattered,

or that the pain didn't shape me.

It's remembering without being ruled by the memory.

I used to grip pain like it gave me identity

proof that I'd loved, that I'd lost, that I had lived.

But all it gave me was weight.

And slowly,

I learned that to heal is to unclench your fists

and release what no longer serves

who you're becoming.

So, I let go— of what they did,

of what I didn't say, of the need to rewrite the past.

I keep the lessons, the strength, the scars

but I leave the heaviness behind.

Because healing isn't about erasing the story.

It's about turning the page

with gentler hands.

Section III: The Garden of Becoming (Growth & Transformation)

This section explores personal growth, letting go, and becoming who you were always meant to be. Like a garden, your soul goes through seasons—planting, pruning, and blooming.

Scriptures:

John 15:2 (NIV) "He cuts off every branch in me that bears no fruit, while every branch that does bear fruit he prunes so that it will be even more fruitful."

2 Corinthians 5:17 (NIV) "Therefore, if anyone is in Christ, the new creation has come: The old has gone, the new is here!"

Philippians 1:6 (NIV) "...He who began a good work in you will carry it on to completion..."

Finding Myself

I spent years chasing approval,

dressing my worth in what others saw,

smoothing every edge of my soul

just to fit into spaces too small for my spirit.

But I got tired of shrinking.

Of pretending. Of dimming my light

to comfort those afraid of their own.

One day, I stopped running.

I turned inward.

And there—beneath the debris of doubt,

the ashes of lost dreams I found him.

The man I abandoned for acceptance.

Unapologetic. Whole, Raw and radiant.

Now, I live in the mirror,

not to criticize, but to recognize myself again.

Not the reflection shaped by others,

but the truth I buried under silence.

Finding myself wasn't a single moment.

It was a series of brave choices:

To choose healing over hiding.

Growth over guilt.

Love over fear. And me—finally me—over everything else.

The Journey Within

They told me to search for happiness

in people, places, possessions.

But the farther I wandered,

the more I longed for something deeper

a peace that couldn't be purchased,

a joy not tied to circumstance.

So, I turned inward.

Not because it was easy, but because I had no choice.

My soul was starving for something real.

Inside, I met my pain

unfiltered, unhealed.

I sat with it.

Held it like an old friend.

And it softened.

I found the little boy I used to be,

hiding in the corners of my doubt,

waiting to be heard.

I listened; I wept.

I promised to never leave him again.

The journey within

is the longest road we take.

But it's the only one that ever leads us home.

Unchained Spirit

There was a time I believed

that suffering was survival

that to love was to lose, that strength meant silence.

But I am unlearning.

I am untethering.

Every chain I wore like jewelry

is falling off piece by piece.

I speak now.

Even when my voice shakes.

Even when they say I'm too much,

too loud, too bold.

Because I've spent too many years

chained to the version of me

they were comfortable with.

And he was never truly me.

I am fire and water, calm and stormy,

gentle and fierce.

And I won't apologize for choosing freedom

over familiarity.

Healing from the Hurt

Healing isn't a straight line.

It's a spiral, a stumble, a surrender.

It's waking up some days feeling whole,

and others wondering if you ever truly began.

But I've learned that progress isn't always visible.

Sometimes, it's just the fact

that I didn't cry today.

Or that I said "no" without guilt.

I've stopped rushing.

Stopped comparing my wounds

to anyone else's journey.

Because this path is mine,

and my pain is valid,

even when others don't understand it.

Healing from the hurt isn't about forgetting it happened.

It's about reclaiming the power you once gave away.

And learning, slowly, to love yourself

in the places you once only saw pain.

The Mirror Tells No Lies

I used to avoid mirrors

not because of how I looked,

but because of how I felt.

Empty, Ashamed.

Like a stranger lived behind my eyes.

But now, I stare straight into the glass.

I meet the man I've become

with grace, not judgment.

The mirror doesn't lie.

It shows the bags under my eyes

from sleepless nights.

The curve of a mouth

that's whispered both prayers and curses.

Eyes that have seen too much but still shine.

What I see now is resilience in skin,

faith in flaws, and beauty

not in perfection—but in the courage

to still stand tall after being broken.

The Power of Self-Worth

They can't take from me

what I've already claimed.

Not anymore.

I used to measure my value

by their treatment of me—

as if their love defined my lovability,

as if rejection meant I was unworthy.

But I've tasted something stronger now:

the quiet certainty that I am enough.

No more begging to be chosen.

No more shrinking for space.

No more tying my joy to someone else's approval.

I am the prize.

The peace.

The promise I made to myself

to never forget my own value again.

Self-worth isn't arrogance.

It's truth.

It's freedom.

And it's mine.

One Foot In, One Foot Out

I lived like that for years—

half healed, half hiding.

One foot in the fire,

one foot chasing freedom.

I wanted to change but feared the cost.

I desired love but ran from closeness.

I spoke of growth

but clung to pain like a blanket.

But healing doesn't happen

when you only visit wholeness.

It demands commitment.

A full surrender.

So, I chose.

I stepped all the way in.

Into the discomfort.

Into the unknown.

Into the truth

that I am not the pain I survived,

but the person who rose from it.

Now, I live with both feet

planted in purpose.

Escaping the Shadows

The shadows followed me even in sunlight

whispers of doubt, flickers of fear.

But I learned they had no power

I didn't give them.

So, I stopped running.

I faced them.

Sat in their darkness

and asked them why they lingered.

And they told me:

"We are only here

because you believed

you weren't enough."

Now I walk

not without fear,

but with faith bigger than fear.

I've learned to cast my own light.

And though the shadows still exist,

They no longer define me.

I escaped, not by outrunning them

but by no longer believing their lies.

Survival vs. Love

I used to think love meant survival

clinging, sacrificing, hurting in silence

just to stay connected.

But survival isn't love.

It's fear wearing a mask.

And I wore it well

until I forgot what joy felt like.

Now, I know love doesn't suffocate.

It breathes life.

It sees me fully and still stays.

I no longer choose what drains me.

I choose what heals.

Because I deserve more

than just surviving.

I deserve peace, presence,

and the kind of love

that doesn't demand

I lose myself to keep it.

A Letter to My Past Self

Dear me,

You did the best you could with what you knew.

And I forgive you

for the times you let yourself down

just to lift others up.

I forgive the silence when you should've spoken.

The tears you hid.

The love you gave to people who didn't return it.

You were just trying to be whole

in a world that kept breaking you.

But look at you now.

Wiser, Softer, Stronger.

You made it through nights you thought would kill you.

You rose from ashes even when no one clapped.

Thank you

for surviving long enough to meet this version of us

the one who finally knows

that healing is holy,

and we were always worthy of it.

Section IV: The Weight of Love (Heartbreak & Healing)

This section explores the beauty and the burden of love, how it breaks us, teaches us, and ultimately heals us. It speaks to heartbreak, grief, letting go, and the holy act of starting over.

Scriptures:

Psalm 34:18 (NIV) "The Lord is close to the brokenhearted and saves those who are crushed in spirit."

1 Corinthians 13:7 (NIV) "Love always protects, always trusts, always hopes, always perseveres."

Ecclesiastes 3:4 (NIV) "...a time to weep and a time to laugh, a time to mourn and a time to dance."

Echoes of a Fading Soul

There's a quiet that comes

before the end— not silence,

but a soft unraveling.

Like the last note of a song

lingering in the air, trying not to disappear.

I have felt that quiet in hospital rooms,

in whispered prayers,

in the moment someone breathes out and never back in.

We are here and then we are not.

And everything we once held

becomes memory, becomes dust.

But I've learned this:

A soul doesn't vanish— It echoes.

In the laughter of children,

in the scent of worn sweaters,

in the stories we tell

and retell to keep the love alive.

So, when I go, don't just mourn me— listen.

Listen for the echo.

You'll find me there,

where love refuses to die.

Living & Leaving

We are born with no concept of time

just wonder, just breath.

But somewhere along the way

we begin to measure everything:

Years, losses, accomplishments, regrets.

We fear leaving so much

We forget to live.

But life isn't in how long we last

It's in how deep we love, how loudly we laugh,

how bravely we forgive.

When my time comes, I don't want a perfect eulogy.

I want people to say:

"He made the moments matter."

"He danced while the music played."

"He didn't wait for forever

he lived like today was his only chance."

Because maybe it is.

A Conversation with Death

I met Death one night,

not in fear, but in curiosity.

I asked, "Why do you come like a thief?"

Death replied,

"Because you treat life like a guarantee."

"Why do you take the good ones early?"

Death answered,

"Because time doesn't measure worth—only passing."

I sat with Death, not as an enemy, but as a mirror.

And I realized: It's not Death we fear

It's the life we haven't fully lived,

the words we've left unsaid,

the love we didn't give

because we thought there was more time.

But there isn't always.

So I thanked Death

for reminding me to live.

Regret: The Last Breath

No one lies on their deathbed

wishing they worked more,

that they chased more money,

or held more grudges.

It's the "I love you" they didn't say.

The apology that stayed stuck

in the throat.

The hug they refused to give

out of pride.

Regret is the breath you try to catch

when it's too late.

So, while you have time

say it. Do it.

Forgive them.

Forgive yourself.

Because when the curtain falls,

you don't want your final act to be silence.

Dying Young, Dying Old

Some leave early

a candle snuffed out

before it could fully burn.

Others stay too long,

watching the world forget

who they used to be.

But whether we go

in our twenties

or our nineties,

the truth remains the same:

Every day is a fragile gift.

And none of us knows

if we're in the beginning,

the middle, or the last line

of our story.

So, don't wait

for a diagnosis

or disaster

to wake you up.

Live like you know

that time isn't promised,

and neither is tomorrow.

The Cost of Time

Time doesn't ask for permission.

It doesn't knock.

It doesn't pause

when we beg it to.

It moves

tireless, ruthless,

and always forward.

We trade time for comfort,

for careers,

for approval.

But rarely do we ask:

Is the cost worth it?

We spend time

like it's infinite,

never realizing

It's the most expensive thing we own.

When you look back,

will your hours be receipts

for things that didn't matter?

Or will your time

tell a story worth remembering?

Goodbye

Goodbye is a word that never sits right on the tongue.

It tastes of loss, of letting go,

of love with nowhere left to go.

But sometimes it's not a door closing

it's a hand releasing,

trusting that what we had

was enough.

I've said goodbye

to people I wasn't ready to lose.

To versions of me I outgrew.

To dreams that didn't fit anymore.

And though each goodbye

has carved something out of me,

It also made room

for something new.

So, here's to courage

to say goodbye

when we must

and the hope

that in every ending

there's a beginning,

waiting to unfold.

What We Take for Granted

We walk past miracles every day

sunsets, heartbeat rhythms,

voices calling our name.

We rush, we complain,

we plan for futures as if now isn't sacred.

Until something stops us.

A loss. A scare. A whisper from the grave

reminding us that this breath

might be the last we ever take for granted.

Don't wait until the funeral

to appreciate a soul.

Don't wait until the silence

to hear what was once spoken.

Love out loud.

Forgive faster.

And be present while you still can.

Living to Impress, Dying Unfulfilled

We perform, we post, we chase likes

instead of light.

We bury our truths beneath expectations,

trading authenticity for applause.

And when the curtain closes,

who were we really?

The version they adored?

Or the self we silenced to fit in?

I don't want to die having only existed

in other people's eyes.

I want to live

wild, flawed, honest

with purpose over performance,

peace over popularity.

Let them talk.

Let them misunderstand.

As long as you die

having truly lived.

The Final Whisper

When it's my time,

don't mourn with heavy hearts.

Don't clothe yourselves in black

as if I've vanished.

I will be the whisper in the wind,

the hush before sunrise,

the pause between your heartbeat and a memory.

I won't be gone I'll be folded

into every sacred thing

that ever made you feel alive.

In the tears you cry,

know that love left behind

never dies. And if you listen

really listen

you'll hear me.

In the rustle of trees,

in the stillness of night,

in the breath of your soul

when you say my name...

That's where I'll be.

Forever echoing in love's eternal whisper.

Section V: Devotion and Depth (Spiritual Intimacy)

This section dives deep into sacred love—be it with God, a partner, or your own inner self. It speaks of intimacy, reverence, and the beauty of staying when it's easier to run.

Scriptures:

Psalm 63:1 (NIV) "You, God, are my God, earnestly I seek you; I thirst for you..."

Song of Solomon 8:7 (NIV) "Many waters cannot quench love; rivers cannot sweep it away."

James 4:8 (NIV) "Come near to God, and He will come near to you."

A Father's Promise

I made a promise the day you came in my life

not with words, but with my soul.

To guard you, Guide you,

and be the arms you run to

when the world feels too loud.

I may not always know the right things to say,

but I will always show up.

Even in my silence,

I hope you feel the roar of my love

echoing through every sacrifice.

You carry my name,

but you'll make your own.

And when you fall,

know this:

You'll never fall alone.

My love isn't perfect,

but it's unwavering.

And if I leave this world before I've said it enough

remember this promise:

As long as breath ever lived in me,

I was yours.

Roots That Run Deep

Our bloodline is more than history

it's spirit, it's survival,

it's strength passed down

in lullabies and lectures,

in recipes and rituals,

in names whispered like prayers.

We were never just born

we were planted.

Rooted in faith, weathered by storms,

nourished by love and loss.

Every wrinkle in Grandma's hands is a story.

Every scar our fathers carry

was earned.

Every "I love you" we didn't know how to say

was still felt.

Legacy isn't gold

it's grit.

It's family showing up

when the world shuts down.

It's roots that run deep,

so we can grow and never forget

where we came from.

The Strength of a Name

I carry a name etched in history

a tapestry of sweat, pain, and perseverance.

A name shaped by fathers who bled for dignity,

by mothers who bent but never broke,

by ancestors who prayed under stars

and hoped their children would one day rise.

This name isn't just mine

it's a badge, a burden, a blessing.

Every time I sign it,

I honor the ones who couldn't.

Every time I speak it,

I speak for those whose voices were silenced.

May I walk with pride, not arrogance.

With purpose, not performance.

Because this name

was not given lightly

it was earned in the fire.

And I intend to pass it on

stronger than it came to me.

Grandma's Unbreakable Love

Her hands tell stories of decades gone by

wrinkled maps of wisdom,

calloused from holding too much sorrow

and never letting go.

She loved without limits, gave without measure.

Discipline came with a hug, a prayer,

a plate of food that healed more than hunger.

Her house was sanctuary,

her voice—gospel.

She could command a room

with silence, and raise generations

with nothing but faith

and soul food.

Now that she's gone, Her love lingers.

In the softness of my own hands,

in the way I hold my children close,

in the warmth that fills the room

when I whisper her name.

Some angels never grow wings- they grow gardens,

cook meals and raise legacies.

A Mother's Pain

She carried more than children

she carried burdens

too heavy for one soul, but bore them with grace.

The world saw her smile,

but I saw the tears she saved for the pillow

when no one was watching.

She poured herself out,

hoping we'd never feel

what she silently endured.

She went without,

so we could grow with.

She held in heartbreak,

so we could hold onto hope.

Motherhood is sacrifice

with no applause,

pain wrapped in patience,

love stitched through sleepless nights.

To every mother hiding her tears

behind bedtime stories—

your pain is seen.

And your love has already saved generations.

The Weight of a Father's Shoulders

He doesn't always say much

but the world rests on his back.

Bills, burdens, broken dreams

he bears them all

so his children don't have to.

He walks through storms

with silence,

because being strong is the only option

they left him.

But inside, he remembers what it was like

to be a boy

longing for a father's love that never came.

So, he overcompensates

shows up at games, sits in parent meetings,

teaches his son to shave

and his daughter to stand tall.

He may not say "I love you" often,

but he says it in sacrifices.

In early mornings, in long hours, In never giving up.

That's the weight A real father carries

and he lifts it like a king.

Lessons Passed Down

I didn't learn from books.

I learned from watching

from the way my mother moved

like music even when life felt like static.

I learned from my father's hands

how they built and broke and built again.

From Grandma's stories,

from Grandpa's quiet strength,

from uncles who drank too much

but still loved deeply,

and aunts who held the family together

with gospel and grit.

The lessons weren't written they were lived.

And now it's my turn.

To pass down more than words

to pass down presence.

To be the shoulder, the example, the legacy

They were to me.

For the Ones Who Raised Me

This is for the ones who didn't have much

but gave everything.

Who taught me that love

isn't loud, but consistent.

That respect is earned

through presence, not power.

They gave me morals in their quiet way.

Taught me how to pray, how to fight without fists,

how to speak truth even when it trembled.

They weren't perfect but they were present.

And in a world that's so quick to leave,

that's everything.

So, if I rise, if I build, if I become

know it's because of them.

Their fingerprints are all over my future.

The Unseen Sacrifices

There are things they never told us

nights they went hungry so, we could eat,

tears cried in silence so, we could sleep in peace.

The dreams they buried

so we could chase ours,

the pain they swallowed

so we wouldn't taste it.

They showed up to everything

even when they were falling apart.

We'll never know

half the sacrifices made behind the scenes.

But we can honor them

not just with gratitude, but with action.

By becoming the peace

they never had.

By living the dreams they never could.

That's how we repay the silent love that built us.

Family: The Blood That Binds Us

We fight, we cry, we drift, we return.

But in the end— We are family.

Bound not just by blood, but by moments.

Sunday dinners, shared secrets, silent forgiveness.

Family isn't perfect it's persistence.

It's choosing each other

again and again, even when it's hard.

We are held together by names,

by roots, by a love that stretches

across time and mistakes.

We may change, We may fall,

but we rise together.

Because no matter where life takes us,

home is where our hearts first learned to beat

in rhythm with one another.

Section VI: The Voice Within (Identity & Empowerment)

This section calls you to remember who you are, your worth, your power, your truth. It breaks chains of doubt and insecurity, empowering you to stand boldly in your light.

Scriptures:

Jeremiah 1:5 (NIV) "Before I formed you in the womb I knew you, before you were born, I set you apart…"

2 Timothy 1:7 (NIV) "For the spirit God gave us does not make us timid, but gives us power, love, and self-discipline."

Romans 8:37 (NIV) "In all these things we are more than conquerors through Him who loved us."

A Black Man's Burden

To be a Black man in this world

is to carry a weight you never agreed to lift

a burden inherited before you ever knew your own name.

They judge you before you speak,

fear you before you move,

limit you before you even dream.

You are asked to be strong

without ever being nurtured,

to lead without ever being led,

to rise while being chained.

But still— you rise.

You walk tall even when the world tries to make you crawl.

You love even when you were taught to survive, not feel.

The burden is real.

But so is the brilliance, the beauty, the resilience.

You are not what they expect—

you are everything they fear.

A Black man who knows his worth

is revolution incarnate.

The Streets Keep Calling

The streets don't whisper— they scream.

They offer escape with a loaded price tag.

Some kids grow up with lullabies,

others with sirens.

Some inherit homes, others inherit survival instincts.

The streets raise many because fathers didn't.

They offer identity, protection, brotherhood

even if all of it's wrapped in danger.

The trap ain't just a place

it's a mindset.

One foot in, one foot out,

always feeling like you're drowning

while pretending to float.

But I see the ones who break free

who turn pain into purpose,

who turn the streets into a lesson, not a legacy.

The streets may call— but you don't always have to answer.

You're allowed to choose peace

over pride, purpose over pressure,

and freedom over the familiar.

The Cost of Survival

We weren't taught how to live—

we were taught how to survive.

Keep your head down, don't speak unless spoken to,

trust no one.

Survival is exhausting.

It's waking up in fight-or-flight,

wondering if today you'll be a statistic, a mugshot, a mural.

They think we're cold, but they don't know

we've buried emotions just to stay sane.

They don't see the brilliance in us

because they're too busy studying our brokenness.

But survival isn't all we are

we are poets, kings, architects, dreamers with callused hearts.

We didn't choose struggle

but we're mastering the art of thriving anyway.

And even if survival has a cost, so does silence.

And we refuse to pay that one.

Gun Violence in Milwaukee

Another candlelight vigil.

Another name etched on a T-shirt.

Another family broken

echoes of gunshots still ringing in their dreams.

In Milwaukee, The headlines don't shock us anymore.

They numb us.

Make us immune to grief, to loss,

to the slow bleeding of a community.

We don't just mourn bodies

we mourn futures.

Graduations that won't happen,

first loves that end in funerals,

mothers who scream at the sky with nothing left to give.

But it's deeper than guns

it's poverty, Its trauma,

It's a system that built cages faster than classrooms.

Still, we hope. Still, we fight.

Still, we pray for peace

in neighborhoods where peace has become a myth.

Milwaukee is bleeding—but not broken.

And we still believe that healing is possible.

The Forgotten Souls of Our City

They walk past them like shadows on concrete.

Men who once had dreams, women who once had homes,

children who never had a chance.

We call them "homeless" but they are human.

Souls stitched with sorrow, stories we never stop to hear.

Addiction doesn't make you less.

Poverty doesn't erase your worth.

Mental illness is not a crime.

But society acts like it is.

We judge their torn clothes,

but ignore the torn systems that put them there.

And in our rush to "move forward,"

We leave behind the very heart of the city

the ones who once built it, loved it, died for it.

If you want to measure a city's soul,

don't count buildings.

Count how many forgotten people

still manage to smile

even when the world looks away.

The Price of Being a Black Man

The price of being a Black man is being seen as a threat

before you're seen as human.

It's being pulled over for fitting a description.

It's being followed in stores

because they fear your skin more than their own reflection.

It's dying for walking, for breathing, for simply existing

in a place that wasn't built to hold your greatness.

It's pressure to be perfect just to be accepted.

To succeed twice as hard to be seen half as worthy.

But still— we laugh, we love, we lead.

We rise from ashes again, and again.

Because though the price is high,

the value of who we are is even higher.

And no amount of oppression can cancel a purpose

carved by God Himself.

Police Brutality: A Stolen Breath

He said, "I can't breathe." And the world watched

as if pain had become performance.

His breath was stolen— but so was our peace.

So was our illusion that justice could be blind

when it's always been selective.

How many knees must crush necks before the world listens?

How many mothers must bury sons

who never made it home from a simple walk?

We're tired of hashtags.

Tired of waiting for the system to fix

what it was designed to break. But still, we protest.

Still, we speak names that should have lived longer.

Because silence is complicity.

And every breath we still have is a vow—

to demand change until no more air is stolen.

The Weight of the World on Our Shoulders

We carry too much. Expectations.

Generational trauma. The unspoken rule:

"Don't let them see you struggle."

We are sons of strength, daughters of defiance,

walking through fire with no map, just memory.

And still they wonder why we break down.

Why we grow quiet.

Why we numb ourselves just to feel normal.

But it's not weakness— It's fatigue.

From being everything to everyone

while still trying to figure out who we are.

Yet here we are—standing, loving. leading.

The weight is heavy, but we are heavier with purpose.

And no weight can crush a soul that refuses to fold.

Black Men, We Must Do Better

My brothers— we are kings.

But kings who sometimes forget

how to build thrones instead of trauma.

We've been hurt—

yes.

But we cannot use pain as permission

to become what broke us.

We must protect our women

as fiercely as we protect our pride.

We must raise our sons

with presence, not excuses.

We must heal— not hide.

Accountability is not betrayal— it's rebirth.

And our community depends on us

to stop normalizing what's killing us.

So, let's talk, let's cry, let's lead, let's learn.

Because if we want better, we must become better.

Not perfect—but present, whole, real.

And that's how we start a revolution.

The Revolution Within

Change won't come from the outside in.

It begins with the man in the mirror,

the woman behind the pain,

the child who still dreams.

Revolution isn't just marching— it's mentoring.

It's healing. It's breaking cycles

with courage and consistency.

They fear our fists,

but they should fear our minds.

Our art, our unity. our refusal to disappear.

Let your life be your loudest protest.

Let your healing be your greatest resistance.

We don't need permission to rise.

We need conviction to begin.

The system may be flawed— but so were we.

And still we chose to grow.

The revolution begins within.

Section VII: Divine Whispers (Faith & Spirituality)

The final section is a return to God—the source of peace, strength, and grace. These poems are prayers, declarations, and sacred reminders that no matter what we face, God is present, near, and faithful.

Scriptures:

Isaiah 30:21 (NIV) "Whether you turn to the right or to the left, your ears will hear a voice behind you, saying, 'This is the way; walk in it.'"

Psalm 91:1 (NIV) "Whoever dwells in the shelter of the Most High will rest in the shadow of the Almighty."

Romans 8:28 (NIV) "And we know that in all things God works for the good of those who love Him..."

When God Found Me

I didn't find God— He found me.

Not in a church pew, not in a Sunday robe,

but in the silence between my sobs,

in the rubble of my mistakes.

He met me in the midnight hour

when I couldn't pray pretty prayers.

When I said, "Lord, I'm tired,"

and meant every syllable

from the marrow of my pain.

He didn't demand perfection.

He didn't shame me for the mess I was.

He just opened His arms

and said, "I never left you."

That kind of love— that kind of grace

isn't earned. It's poured.

Now, I walk not because I'm strong,

but because He carries me.

I speak not because I'm wise,

but because He whispers truth into my soul.

When God found me, I finally saw who I really was

not what the world called me, but what He always knew:

Chosen. Worthy. Redeemed.

Whispers in the Stillness

Sometimes, God doesn't thunder.

He whispers.

He doesn't part seas— He calms storms within.

We keep looking for miracles in the dramatic,

but often miss Him in the daily breath,

the quiet peace, the moment of clarity

when all chaos slows.

He speaks when you sit still.

When the phone is down.

When the world fades and it's just you and Him.

That whisper? It's your reminder.

That you are loved.

That you are held.

That even in the silence, you are seen.

So don't rush the stillness.

Don't fear the quiet.

That's where the Spirit moves.

That's where the healing begins.

That's where you remember

God has never stopped speaking.

You just had to be still enough to hear.

Faith That Walks Through Fire

I've walked through fires
that should've burned me whole. I've been in valleys
where the shadows tried to bury me. But I'm still standing
not because I'm strong, but because faith refused to fold.
Faith isn't the absence of fear. It's walking while afraid.
It's trusting what you can't see,
believing what hasn't happened,
and praising while the tears are still falling.
It's saying, "Even if the mountain doesn't move,
I will still climb."
Because I know my God.
Not the God of comfort,
but the God of deliverance.
The One who shows up in furnaces
and says, "Not today, fire—this one is Mine."
So, no matter what I face—
I walk with Him.
Even through fire, even through storms,
even when the world says,
"Give up."
My faith says, "Go forward."

I Am Not Alone

There were nights

when loneliness sat heavy on my chest.

Mornings where the silence screamed.

I looked around and saw no one

but somehow, I made it through.

Because I was never alone.

God was there

when friends vanished. He was near

when I didn't even have the strength to say His name.

He was the warmth in cold rooms,

the hand that caught mine

when I was slipping.

It took me time to realize His presence

wasn't always loud.

Sometimes, it was a breath, a feeling,

a verse I needed at just the right time.

I'm not alone, never was, never will be.

His love is constant.

His presence is personal.

And His silence is never absence.

A Prayer for the Wounded

Lord, this prayer is for the broken.

For the ones smiling in public

but bleeding in private.

For the ones holding on by threads and whispers.

Touch them, hold them.

Remind them they're still whole in You.

Lift the shame. Soften the scars.

Let them know they don't have to pretend

in Your presence. You see the soul

beneath the struggle. You see the heart behind the walls.

Send peace that passes understanding.

Send healing that touches what therapy couldn't reach.

Send grace that rewrites every label.

God, wrap Your arms around every wounded soul tonight.

And let them know— they are loved.

They are worthy, they are Yours.

Amen.

God of the Second Chance

If grace had a name, it would be Second Chance.

Because I've messed up— again, and again.

Walked away, doubted, got tired, chose wrong.

But God never flinched. Never withdrew.

He just kept waiting—arms wide, eyes full of mercy.

He doesn't write us off. He writes us back in.

That's the kind of love you don't find in people.

Only in God.

He doesn't just forgive— He restores.

He doesn't just wipe your slate clean—

He writes something new on it.

So, if you feel too far gone— you're not.

There's still a door open.

Still a seat at the table. Still a God

who believes in the beauty of beginning again.

Strength in Surrender

I used to think surrender meant weakness.

Letting go? That felt like failure.

But then I realized— real strength

is in releasing what you can't control.

Real peace is in saying,

"God, You lead."

I don't have to carry it all.

I was never meant to.

He's the Shepherd— I'm the sheep.

He's the Way— I just walk it.

And every time I release it—

the fear, the pride, the pressure—

He replaces it with something greater: rest.

So now, I surrender

not as a victim, but as a victor

who knows that letting go is how I rise.

My Heart Belongs to God

You can have my heart, Lord.

All of it.

The parts that still ache,

the parts that still wonder,

the parts that shine.

This world tried to claim it

but I'm giving it back

to the One who made it.

You know every corner of me.

You know the secrets, the storms,

the stories I've buried.

And still—You love me.

So, I give You my praise,

even when life hurts.

I give You my yes,

even when I don't understand.

I give You my heart

because no one's ever held it

as gently as You.

Built by Grace

I am not self-made. I am grace-built.

Every open door—grace.

Every closed one—grace, too.

Every lesson I survived,

every battle I won

not by my strength,

but by His mercy.

I've seen storms calm

at the sound of His name.

I've seen dead dreams rise

when I put them back in His hands.

So don't look at me and see luck. See grace.

I am a product of His patience,

a result of His relentless love.

He never gave up on me— not once.

And now I live,

not just to succeed,

but to glorify the One

who never stopped believing in me.

Whispers of the Soul

There is a voice beneath the silence, a murmur in the marrow of midnight,

where unspoken dreams gather like dust in the corners of a weary heart.

It speaks in sighs between heartbeats, in the tremble of hands longing for touch,

in the echoes of names we dare not call but still carry like sacred scripture.

It is the hush of love never returned, the prayer caught in the throat of the broken,

the lullaby of ghosts that never left, rocking in the cradle of memory.

It is the weight of a father's regret, the ache of a mother's empty arms,

the longing of a soul too heavy to fly, yet too restless to stay buried in flesh.

The soul does not shout; it does not beg to be heard. It whispers.

Soft as the wind through an open window, gentle as the hands of time tracing our scars,

patient as the sky waiting for dawn. Listen.

Beneath the noise of the world, beneath the armor you wear,

Beneath the war in your mind— your soul is speaking.

Not in words, but in feeling. Not in sound, but in knowing.

Close your eyes. Be still. And let the whispers guide you home.

Reflections & Scriptures

Spiritual Meditations for Each Section of Volume I: Whispers of the Soul

Section I: Echoes of the Heart

Theme: Love, passion, heartbreak, devotion.

1 Corinthians 13:4–7 (NIV)

"Love is patient, love is kind... It always protects, always trusts, always hopes, always perseveres."

Song of Solomon 8:6 (KJV)

"Set me as a seal upon thine heart... for love is strong as death."

Reflection:

Love leaves echoes in the soul—some soft, some aching, all sacred. Whether it lifts you or breaks you, love teaches you how deeply your heart can feel.

Section II: Scars & Shadows

Theme: Pain, loss, mental battles, emotional wounds.

Psalm 147:3 (KJV)

"He healeth the broken in heart, and bindeth up their wounds."

Isaiah 43:2 (KJV)

"When thou passest through the waters, I will be with thee..."

Reflection:

Even shadows require light to exist. And every scar is proof you survived what tried to break you. You are still here—for a reason.

Section III: Roads to Redemption

Theme: Growth, self-discovery, resilience, healing.

Psalms 139:23-24 (ESV)

"Search me, O God, and know my heart! Try me and know my thoughts! And see if there be any grievous way in me, and lead me in the way everlasting!"

Jeremiah 30:17 (ESV)

"For I will restore health to you, and your wounds I will heal, declares the lord."

Reflection:

Healing isn't a destination—it's a road. One paved with self-awareness, surrender, and faith. You're not lost—you're becoming.

Section IV: Life's Fragile Dance

Theme: Mortality, regret, time, life and death.

Psalms 90:12 (ESV)

"So teach us to number our days that we may get a heart of wisdom."

Ecclesiastes 3:1-2 (ESV)

"For everything there is a season, and a time for every matter under heaven: a time to be born, and a time to die

John 10:10 (ESV)

"The Thief comes only to steal and kill and destroy. I came that they may have life and have it abundantly."

Reflection:

Life moves like breath—precious, fleeting. Embrace it with intention. Mourn its losses. Celebrate its moments. And never waste what can't be regained: time.

Section V: Seeds of the Soul

Theme: Family, legacy, lineage, parenthood, ancestral roots.

Proverbs 22:6 (KJV)

"Train up a child in the way he should go: and when he is old, he will not depart from it."

Deuteronomy 6:6–7 (KJV)

"These words... shall be in thine heart: and thou shalt teach them diligently unto thy children."

Psalms 145:4 (ESV)

"One generation shall commend your works to another, and shall declare your mighty acts."

Reflection:

Family is the soil where your soul was planted. You are someone's answered prayer, someone's sacrifice, someone's legacy. Make your roots proud.

Section VI: Fire & Fury

Theme: Societal injustice, racial struggle, survival, truth.

Isaiah 1:17 (KJV)

"Learn to do well; seek judgment, relieve the oppressed, judge the fatherless, plead for the widow."

Amos 5:24 (KJV)

"But let justice roll down like waters, and righteousness like a mighty stream."

Psalms 103:6 (ESV)

"The Lord works righteousness and justice for all who are oppressed."

Reflection:

To cry out for justice is not rebellion—it is righteousness. Your voice is divine. Your pain is sacred. And your truth is a weapon against silence.

Section VII: Divine Whispers

Theme: Faith, salvation, redemption, spiritual peace.

Psalm 46:10 (KJV)

"Be still, and know that I am God..."

Isaiah 40:31 (KJV)

"But they that wait upon the Lord shall renew their strength..."

Reflection:

God does not always speak in thunder. Sometimes, He whispers—in the stillness, in the surrender, in the broken places. Listen closely. Your spirit already knows His voice.

Reader's Prayer

("A Whisper Back to You")

Dear God,

For the one who has made it to this final page

Let them know You were listening the entire time.

With every poem they read, with every tear they didn't explain,

You were there. Whispering truth. Holding their wounds.

Mending what the world tried to break.

I pray that love has touched them—whether it healed or hurt

And that in the echoes of their own heart,

They heard You whisper back:

"You are worthy, even when you don't feel it."

May every scar remind them they're still alive.

May every shadow teach them where to find the light.

And may every seed planted by these words bloom

Into compassion, courage, and clarity.

Lord, wrap this reader in peace.

Fill the cracks in their soul with grace.

Give them rest where they've been restless,

And vision where they've been blind.

Let them leave this book not just as a reader,

But as a soul reborn in truth.

Amen.

"Only in the silence of the soul's deepest cry do we hear the voice of God most clearly."

—K.C.

Romans 8:26 (NIV)

"The Spirit helps us in our weakness. For we do not know what we ought to pray for, but the Spirit Himself intercedes for us through wordless groans."

Section I: The Cry Beneath the Silence

Theme: Hidden pain, silent suffering, emotional suppression.

Section 1: There are aches so deep, words fail to name them. There are tears we swallow whole, griefs we carry in silence. This section speaks for the soul that has wept in the dark, the heart that smiled in public while breaking secrets. These are the cries heard only by heaven

Psalm 34:18 (KJV)

"The Lord is nigh unto them that are of a broken heart; and saveth such as be of a contrite spirit."

Romans 8:26 (NIV)

"Likewise the Spirit also helpeth our infirmities: for we know not what we should pray for as we ought: but the Spirit itself maketh intercession for us with groanings which cannot be uttered."

The Cry I Never Spoke

I held it in— not because I was strong,

but because I didn't know how to let it out without falling apart.

There were no words for the ache in my chest,

no language for the weight of waking up every day and pretending I was whole.

I smiled, and it was convincing.

Laughed, and it echoed through empty halls

where no one knew my joy had packed up and left.

At night, I talked to the ceiling. Not even a prayer,

just the silence of a soul trying to breathe

beneath the rubble of unspoken sorrow.

I learned how to bury pain beneath productivity.

To clothe my emptiness in good intentions and tight schedules,

as if healing was a task I could check off.

But deep down— there was always that cry.

The one I never spoke, the one that never made it past my throat,

the one only God could hear when my lips stayed still

but my soul screamed for mercy. And somehow, He did hear it.

In the silence, In the stillness. He reached for the pain

I thought no one saw.

And maybe that's what saved me— not the strength to speak,

but the grace of a God who listens to tears

even when they never fall.

Tears Behind the Eyes

Some tears don't fall. They sit behind the eyes

like a storm that never breaks— heavy, waiting,

too proud or too afraid to let go.

You've seen them before— in the stare of a tired woman

who's given all her love to people who forgot to love her back.

In the silent nod of a man who's learned to choke down sorrow

because boys were never taught how to cry and still be men.

They hide in the tight jaw, the swallowed words,

the fake "I'm fine" said with just enough breath

to keep people from asking again.

Tears behind the eyes don't need an audience.

They just need space— somewhere sacred where the soul can unclench

and let what's hidden finally rise. God sees those tears. The invisible ones.

The ones we hold back out of pride or pain or survival.

He sees them when no one else does, counts them like sacred offerings,

bottles them like wine from the crushed vineyard of your heart.

And when the world can't be bothered to ask if you're okay,

He does. Not with words, but with presence.

Not with noise, but with knowing.

Because the tears behind the eyes are loud in heaven.

And even what you hide Is holy in His hands.

The Silence Between My Prayers

There were nights when I prayed and the words felt like whispers
falling into an endless void— no echo, no answer, just silence.
Not the comforting kind, but the kind that makes you question
if anyone's really listening. The kind that makes you wonder
if heaven turned its face while you knelt in your despair.
I didn't doubt God's power— I doubted my worth.
I wondered if my brokenness made my prayers less worthy,
if the cracks in my faith caused His silence.
But over time, I learned that silence doesn't mean absence.
That sometimes, God doesn't speak
because He's holding me closer than words can reach.
That in the pause between my weeping and His answer,
something sacred is happening. In the silence between my prayers,
He was mending what I didn't even know was torn.
Stretching my patience so, my spirit could grow roots.
Letting the quiet press in so, I'd learn to listen, not just speak.
I used to think silence meant I was alone.
Now I know it means he's doing something deeper—
beneath the noise, beneath the ache, in the stillest part of my soul
where words fail and only trust remains. So, I sit in that silence now, not afraid.
Because I know He's there too— working, waiting, loving me
between the prayers I thought He'd forgotten.

What My Smile Doesn't Say

My smile is well-trained. It arrives on cue,

shining just enough to make you believe I'm okay.

It nods through pain, grins past exhaustion,

and stretches wide enough to hide the cracks behind my eyes.

But there's so much it doesn't say.

It doesn't tell you about the nights I sit in silence,

scrolling through my thoughts like a worn-out journal

with pages too smudged to read.

It doesn't whisper about the mornings I wake up

and have to gather the strength just to face the mirror.

It never speaks of the loneliness that walks beside me in crowded rooms,

how I can be surrounded and still feel unseen.

My smile won't mention the pressure to hold it together

when everything inside is unraveling. It won't confess

how tired I am of being strong for everyone but myself.

But behind it— there's a soul begging to be held without explanation,

to be seen without performing, to be loved without proving It's worth.

God knows what my smile won't say. He sees the sorrow in my silence,

the storm behind my stillness. He doesn't wait for me to put it into words

He just draws near. And in His presence, I don't have to pretend.

I don't have to perform. I don't have to smile just to be believed.

Because with Him, even what's hidden is heard.

The Weight I Carry in Secret

You wouldn't know it by looking at me— how heavy it gets,

this invisible weight I carry through my days.

I've learned how to hide it well, to walk with my back straight

even when my soul stoops under burdens no one else can see.

Some people carry grief like a wound; mine is a whisper

constant, quiet, settled deep beneath my ribs where no one thinks to look.

I laugh on command. I show up, stay strong, and say, "It's all good"

even when it's not. Because admitting the truth

feels like opening a door I may never be able to close.

I carry the weight of expectations, of what I should be by now.

Of who I must be for others. Of what I never had

but was told I should've become. I carry the weight of past pain

that still echoes in new moments, unspoken trauma that rewrites how I love,

how I trust, how I dream. And some days, it gets so loud in my chest that I wonder

how no one else hears it— how I can scream inside

and still be greeted with, "You're so strong." But God knows the weight I carry.

He sees the trembling in my stillness, the shaking in my silence.

He doesn't need a confession to offer comfort.

He just steps in, takes what I can't name, and carries it like it's His own.

He lightens the load without asking for proof. He honors the tears

I never let fall. And that's how I go on—not because the weight disappears,

but because I no longer carry it alone.

The Ache That Has No Name

It doesn't come with a reason. It doesn't ask permission.

It just arrives— this ache I carry, quiet and cold,

settling into my chest like it's lived there all along.

There's no clear memory to point to,

no moment that broke me cleanly in half.

It's a thousand paper cuts from a thousand little hurts,

each one small but together, they bleed something deep.

People ask, "What's wrong?" and I have no answer—

just a shrug, a tight smile, and the echo of something I can't quite explain.

It's not depression, exactly. Not sadness, fully.

It's something in between— a quiet weight, a dull throb,

a feeling that the world is too loud and I'm too tired to keep up.

Sometimes I wonder if I'm just too sensitive,

too soft for a world that praises hard hearts and fast healing.

But then I remember— even Jesus wept.

Even He sat in sorrow so deep, He bled from His skin.

God knows the ache that has no name.

He meets me in the fog where clarity won't come.

He wraps arms of peace around a pain I can't define, and somehow, that's enough.

I may not know why it hurts, but I know I'm not alone in it.

And in that knowing, the ache becomes sacred—

not solved but seen. Not fixed but held.

When I Couldn't Say Help

There were moments I wanted to speak,

but the words lodged in my throat

like stones I couldn't swallow.

Moments I wanted to ask for help,

but pride and pain linked arms and held me hostage.

I rehearsed the plea a hundred times— "I'm not okay."

But something about admitting it

felt like failure. So, I stayed silent,

smiled wider, and wore my hurt like invisible armor.

But inside, I was drowning. Sinking slowly

while everyone complimented how calm the surface looked.

I didn't say "help," but God heard the silence.

He saw the shadows behind my eyes,

read the tremble in my voice when I said I was fine.

He didn't wait for the perfect prayer.

He didn't need the right words.

He came anyway— into the pit, into the fog,

into the locked room where I cried in private.

And I learned something sacred:

you don't always have to speak for heaven to listen.

Even the tears you hide are loud enough for God to move.

Smiling Through Survival

I became a master of pretending—laughing on the outside,

while inside I was breaking quietly, piece by quiet piece.

You'd never know what I was carrying.

I was the one everyone leaned on,

the strong one, the encourager, the fixer.

And maybe I was... but I was also tired. So tired.

It's strange how survival becomes a skill,

how you can live on autopilot so long that pain becomes normal.

But I've learned—there is no trophy for quiet suffering.

No medal for smiling through storms you never told anyone about.

God saw the mask I wore and gently removed it.

He whispered, "You don't have to pretend with Me."

And in that moment, the act ended.

The smile faded, and real healing began.

Not through pretending, but through being seen

exactly as I was—fragile, weary, and worthy of love anyway.

Numb

There was a time when I felt everything too much.

And then, there came a time

when I felt nothing at all.

Numbness crept in like fog—

not loud, not painful, just... silent.

No joy, no sorrow,

just a flatline of feeling

where my heart used to live.

It scared me more than sadness.

Because at least sadness feels.

Numbness is the absence—a soul on pause,

a heart too exhausted to break again.

But even there, God reached for me.

Not with fire, not with fury, but with stillness.

He didn't rush me. He didn't demand I rejoice.

He just sat with me in the in-between.

And slowly, ever so gently, He stirred the waters again.

Not all healing is loud.

Sometimes it's the quiet return

of tears, of laughter, of hope.

I am learning to feel again.

And that, too, is holy.

The Healing in Being Heard

I used to think healing came from fixing the broken pieces,

from solving the problem, from moving on.

But then someone listened—really listened

without rushing to repair, without filling the silence with empty words.

They didn't need to fix me. They just needed to see me.

And in that sacred seeing, a kind of healing began

I didn't know I needed. We talk so much about miracles,

but don't speak enough about the miracle of being heard.

How it feels when someone holds space for your story,

your sorrow, your truth. God does that every day.

He listens when no one else does.

He sits in our silence without judgment, without solutions,

with only love. And maybe healing

isn't always about being "better."

Maybe it's about being known

truly known—and loved anyway.

There's healing in that. A deep, steady kind

that reaches places no sermon ever could.

Section II: Shattered Mirrors

Theme: Identity crises, broken self-image, trauma, confronting shame.

Section II: Shattered Mirrors will explore the deep cracks in identity, self-worth, and emotional reflection. These poems will dive into personal insecurities, inner battles, and the painful truths we often hide from ourselves.

Isaiah 61:1 (KJV)

"He hath sent me to bind up the brokenhearted, to proclaim liberty to the captives, and the opening of the prison to them that are bound."

2 Corinthians 5:17 (KJV)

"Therefore if any man be in Christ, he is a new creature: old things are passed away; behold, all things are become new."

The Mirror Lied to Me

I stood in front of the mirror and asked it who I was.

It stared back, cold and quiet,

showing only what the world had told me to see

flaws, failures, the scars I tried to cover and the dreams I let slip.

It didn't reflect my heart, only the shell.

The surface. The parts they picked apart.

And I believed it. I believed every cruel whisper

the mirror echoed—that I wasn't enough,

wasn't worthy, wasn't beautiful unless someone else said I was.

But the mirror lied to me.

It never showed the love I gave when I was empty.

It didn't show the battles I fought in silence and survived.

It ignored the fire in my soul and the quiet way I rise after every fall.

God, though— He sees beyond the reflection.

He looks through the glass and into the spirit.

He sees me not as broken, but becoming. Not as shameful, but sacred.

And slowly, I'm learning to see me through His eyes.

To touch the cracks in the mirror and not flinch, but marvel

because each one proves I lived, I loved, I learned.

Maybe the mirror doesn't lie—maybe it just doesn't know the whole story yet.

The Me I Hide from Myself

There's a version of me I pretend not to see
the one who questions everything,
who cries in secret and smiles through the pain
just to avoid being a burden.
I keep that version tucked away, behind expectations,
behind toughness, behind all the roles I play so well.
Because if I faced them too long,
I might unravel. And the world doesn't pause for unraveling.
But God sees that version, the hidden me—
the child still afraid of being rejected, the grown soul
still haunted by past mistakes, the one who longs to be held
without being fixed. And instead of turning away, He draws closer.
There's no shame in what He sees.
No disgust in my doubts, no dismissal of my fears.
In His presence, I learn to stop hiding
not just from others, but from myself.
To stand in my full truth and know I'm still loved,
still chosen, still whole.

Cracked but Still Crowned

They tried to strip me of my worth with words like daggers,

with eyes that saw only my flaws. And after a while,

I believed them. I wore my shame like skin,

and forgot I was royal.

But I am not the names they gave me.

Not the failures they never let me forget.

Not the damage they did and blamed me for.

I am cracked—yes. But I'm still crowned.

Still chosen. Still part of a legacy

etched in heaven, not shame.

God didn't wait for me to be polished to call me precious.

He placed the crown on my bowed head

while I was still weeping. And when I doubted,

He whispered, "You are still mine."

A flawed vessel, but filled with glory.

They tried to break me.

But all they did was make room

for God to rebuild me stronger.

What Shame Left Behind

Shame doesn't always shout. Sometimes it whispers,

wraps itself in silence, settles in your skin

like it belongs there. It doesn't just follow you—

it becomes you, until you can't tell the difference

between who you are and what hurt you.

It left me afraid to speak too loud,

to shine too bright, to want too much.

It convinced me I was too much

and never enough, all at once.

But God came for the parts

I thought were ruined.

He gathered my scattered pieces

without judgment, only grace.

He didn't scold me—He soothed me.

Didn't shame me—He sheltered me.

And in His arms,

I learned to leave shame behind.

Not by forgetting,

but by forgiving— myself most of all.

Reflections from a Wounded Soul

I looked in the mirror

and didn't recognize the eyes

staring back.

They were tired, hollow,

silent from too much screaming inside.

I wasn't just wounded— I was still bleeding.

Smiling in public, shattered in private.

Doing just enough to seem okay.

But the soul doesn't lie, not for long.

It aches to be heard, even when it can't speak.

So, I sat with my wounds and listened.

To the pain. To the fear. To the little boy inside

who was still waiting to be chosen.

And there, in that broken silence, God met me.

Not to erase the scars, but to redeem them.

He made my wounds into windows for His light.

The Pieces They Never See

I carry pieces of myself

that never make it into conversation.

The anxious thoughts, the second-guessing,

the old memories that haunt the new moments.

You see my strength—but not the price I paid for it.

You see the smile—but not the moments it cost me.

There are pieces of me I haven't even shown myself.

Buried under survival, silenced by shame,

wrapped in years of "just keep going."

But God is patient. He sits with me

while I peel back layer after layer.

He doesn't flinch. He doesn't rush.

He sees the pieces and calls them holy.

What I thought made me too broken

was what made me most real.

And He blesses even the unseen parts of me.

When I Believed I Wasn't Enough

Somewhere along the way,

I started believing that love had to be earned.

That being myself wasn't good enough

not loud enough, not thin enough, not worthy enough.

I shaped myself to fit into spaces

that were never meant for me.

And called it "growth." But it was really grief.

The grief of shrinking. Of dimming my light

to keep others comfortable.

Of carrying the lie

that I needed to be more to matter.

But God's love doesn't come with conditions.

He doesn't ask me to perform.

He loves the raw me— the real me.

The one who stumbles, doubts, weeps.

He says I'm enough because He made me.

And maybe that's the truth

I'll spend my whole life trying to believe.

The Lie of Perfection

They said be strong.

Be perfect. Be unshakable.

So I tried. And failed.

Perfection became my prison.

Every mistake felt like

a nail in my worth.

Every weakness

like a curse I had to cover.

But no one is born flawless.

Not even the saints.

Even Christ bore wounds—holy scars

that proved love

more than strength ever could.

Perfection isn't the goal.

Wholeness is.

And wholeness means

embracing the parts I wanted to hide—

the messy, the wild, the healing.

God never asked me to be perfect.

He only asked me to be present.

To show up as I am.

And that's enough.

The Mask I Forgot to Take Off

It started small

just a little pretending.

Smile here. Laugh there.

Say "I'm good" when I'm not.

But the mask grew thicker

with each passing day,

until I forgot

how it felt to be bare-faced.

To be honest. I wore it so long,

I started to believe it.

That I had to be "okay" to be accepted.

That the messier parts of me

made people leave.

But God never asked for my mask.

He asked for my heart.

Even when it was heavy.

Even when it was messy.

So I took it off, trembling

afraid of what He'd see.

And He said,

"I've seen it all.

And I still choose you."

Through the Cracks, I Saw God

For so long,

I saw my brokenness

as a curse. A reason to hide.

To stay small. To pretend.

But then one night,

in the middle of my lowest point,

light came through a crack—

just enough to feel it,

not enough to explain it.

It was grace.

Pure and unexpected.

God didn't wait

for me to be whole.

He climbed into the broken pieces

and made a home there.

He didn't fix me first

He loved me first.

And through the cracks, I saw something holy.

Not the end of me, but the beginning of healing.

Now I see my scars

not as shame, but as stained glass— fragile, yes.

But beautiful because light still shines through.

Section III: Dust and Water

Theme: Humility, humanity, rebirth, grace in imperfection.

Section III: Dust and Water will explore the dual nature of our humanity: fragile like dust, yet flowing and resilient like water. These poems will reflect on humility, surrender, emotional cleansing, and the ways we are shaped by both suffering and grace.

Genesis 2:7 (NIV)

"And the Lord God formed man of the dust of the ground, and breathed into his nostrils the breath of life; and man became a living soul."

John 4:14 (KJV)

"But whosoever drinketh of the water that I shall give him shall never thirst…"

Clay in the Potter's Hands

I thought I had to be unbreakable

flawless, polished, untouched by pain.

But I was only clay—soft, scarred, shaping still.

And when I cracked, I feared I'd be discarded,

as if brokenness made me less valuable.

But then God touched me.

Not to throw me away,

but to mold me with mercy.

To press His hands into my fears

and remake me gently.

Each trial was water. Each tear, a tool.

Each silence, a sacred reshaping.

He didn't rush. He didn't force.

He simply turned me in His hands

until the beauty began to rise from the ruins.

Now I no longer fear the process.

Because I know— what He forms, He fills.

And what He fills, He never forsakes.

I am clay. I am His. Still being shaped,

still being seen as worthy.

We Were Made of Dust and Glory

We came from the ground,

from the low and the overlooked—

formed in silence, shaped in shadows.

And yet, God breathed His breath into us.

We are the dust that carries glory.

The soil that shelters Spirit.

So why do we shame our humanity?

Why do we curse our tears,

our longings, our fragile frames?

Even Christ wept.

Even He thirsted.

Even He felt the weight of flesh

and chose not to abandon it.

We were never made to be gods,

but reflections of grace.

Humble vessels

with divine fingerprints.

And the more I embrace

my earthbound soul,

the more I see—

I was never just dust.

I was always holy in His hands.

Baptized by My Own Tears

I used to run from tears,

wiping them away

before they could be seen.

Crying in silence,

like weakness had to hide.

But grief doesn't need shame

it needs space.

Tears don't betray strength—

they birth it. And I learned,

as they fell without end,

that each drop was holy.

Each sob a kind of cleansing.

I baptized myself

in sorrow I once tried to deny.

And from it, I came up different

softer, stronger, honest.

God doesn't waste our water.

He collects every tear

and plants healing in their place.

Now I cry freely, knowing my tears

don't make me less.

They mark my resurrection.

When Water Found My Wounds

It wasn't fire that healed me

not the blaze of pride

or the heat of anger.

It was water, gentle, patient.

It seeped into the wounds

I tried to ignore— the cuts I covered

with busyness and bravado.

And it softened them

without asking for permission.

Water found me

when I couldn't find strength.

It didn't rush. It simply flowed

through me, around me,

cleansing what I thought was permanent.

Sometimes healing is quiet.

It doesn't shout.

It moves like mercy, steady and sacred.

Now I welcome the flow.

The floods.

The rinsing of what was.

Because the water didn't drown me

it delivered me.

Fragile but Full of Faith

I don't always feel strong.

Some days I tremble

under the weight of what I carry.

Some days I question

if I was meant to carry it at all.

But I've learned— faith doesn't always roar.

Sometimes it whispers from a weary soul:

"I still believe." I am fragile. Yes.

But I am full of faith.

And that is enough

for God to work miracles.

He never asked me to be invincible

just available.

To keep showing up

with my cracked heart,

my trembling hands,

my soft voice that still calls His name.

He meets me there,

again and again,

until even my weakness

feels like worship.

Lessons from the River

The river never asks for permission to flow.

It doesn't worry about what it carries—

it just moves.

I watched it one evening,

wishing I could be as free, as sure.

But then I heard God whisper:

"You are the river.

You just forgot."

You've survived floods

and droughts, stones and storms.

And still—you flow.

You've bent without breaking.

Changed course without losing direction.

And the current, though invisible,

has never left you.

There is wisdom in your water.

There is strength

in your softness.

And you don't need permission

to be both deep and wild.

You just need to remember

You were made to move.

The Softening

I used to think

I had to harden to survive.

Build walls. Wear armor.

Keep love and longing

at a safe distance.

But hard things break.

And I was breaking.

So, I asked God to soften me

not to make me weak, but real.

And slowly,

the shell began to crack.

Tears I once swallowed came freely.

Truth I once buried rose like dawn.

It hurt—yes.

But healing often does.

And in that softening,

I found my truest strength.

Not in control, but in surrender.

Not in power, but in presence.

The world told me to be hard.

But God invited me to be whole.

Stillness in the Storm

The waves roared.

The sky darkened.

The storm came loud,

and I was sure

it would take me under.

But in the middle of chaos,

there was stillness.

A voice inside me

that didn't shout—but stayed.

It said, "Be still.

I am here." And suddenly,

the storm didn't feel so powerful.

Because presence

is greater than panic.

I didn't need the storm to stop.

I just needed to remember

who sat in the boat with me.

Even if the waters rise,

even if the thunder shouts,

I am not alone.

And that knowing

is enough to carry me to shore.

The Water Remembers Me

There are parts of me

I forgot. Joy I buried.

Light I dimmed.

Laughter that once danced in open fields.

But the water remembers.

When I stand near the sea,

or sit by a river, I feel it a tug, a tenderness,

like something sacred is calling me home.

It whispers of who I was

before the pain, before the masks,

before the survival.

It speaks to the soul in me

that never stopped flowing.

And I listen. Because maybe

in remembering the water,

I remember myself.

The me that loved freely.

Dreamed boldly.

Believed deeply.

I am still him

just deeper now.

Where Dust Meets Grace

I am not ashamed to be dust.

To admit my limits,

my flaws, my needs.

Dust is not worthless—

it is the starting place

of miracles. And grace?

Grace makes the dust holy.

God didn't breathe life into gold.

He chose dust.

Chose fragility.

Chose the broken thing

to carry the eternal one.

And so I no longer hide my dirt.

I offer it.

I let grace meet it

and make it divine.

In that meeting

dust and grace

I find who I am:

Not perfect.

Not finished.

But gloriously becoming.

Section IV: Songs of the Womb

Theme: Birth, generational connection, motherhood, fatherhood, origin, purpose.

Section IV: Songs of the Womb will be an intimate, powerful exploration of the sacred origin of life—honoring motherhood, fatherhood, creation, the divine feminine, and the quiet strength that begins in the hidden places. This section will echo the heartbeat of legacy, nurturing, and the voice of life even before breath.

Jeremiah 1:5 (KJV)

"Before I formed thee in the belly I knew thee; and before thou camest forth out of the womb I sanctified thee..."

Psalm 127:3 (KJV)

"Lo, children are an heritage of the Lord: and the fruit of the womb is his reward."

Before You Had a Name

Before you had a name, I knew you.

Not in flesh, but in spirit

a quiet flutter in the deep,

a whisper beneath my ribs.

You were promise and prayer,

seed and silence.

And still—you changed everything.

My body became a temple,

my breath a lullaby.

And every heartbeat

carried your becoming.

The world didn't see you,

but I did. In dreams, in cravings,

in the way I held my belly

like a sacred secret. You were mine

before the world could claim you.

Chosen. Cherished.

Held in the place where life begins.

Even now, as you grow beyond my arms,

I remember— the bond was never just skin,

but soul.

You may outgrow my lap, but never my love.

The First Song Was a Mother's Cry

It wasn't a lullaby or a hymn in the night
the first sacred song was a cry.
A deep, aching wail
from a woman becoming a mother.
She cried from pain, from power,
from the soul-splitting moment
where life pushed through her into the world.
That cry echoed through generations
the same sound
when she held her baby for the first time,
when she rocked them through sickness,
when she let go for the first day of school,
and the last day under her roof.
Motherhood isn't quiet.
It sings loud through broken sleep,
through whispered prayers,
through tears that never ask to be seen.
The world calls it instinct. But it's deeper
it's divine.
Because every mother's cry
is sacred music. And in it,
the heavens bend low to listen

My Body Was a Garden

They said I was glowing,

but they didn't see

the sacred war within me.

The stretching, the swelling,

the shifting of spirit and skin.

My body—once my own—

became a garden. And you,

my miracle seed, grew roots in my soul.

I fed you with faith,

watered you with tears,

nurtured you with everything

I didn't know I still had.

I lost myself to become more.

And even now, years later,

when I look at you,

I feel that garden inside me

the bloom I'd bleed for

again and again.

A Father's Voice in the Dark

You won't find him in the spotlight.

You'll find him in the shadows

changing diapers at 3 AM,

whispering prayers over a crib,

silently worrying

how he'll provide.

His voice is steady

when the world is loud.

Firm when needed,

gentle when no one's watching.

A father's love is often a quiet thing

not less powerful, just less praised.

But make no mistake

he is the first hero, the quiet protector,

the steady hands

when life begins to shake.

And when his child cries out,

He comes running

even if it's just a nightmare.

Because a father's voice in the dark

is often the only thing

That makes the fear go away.

Carried in More Than My Womb

You think I carried you

for nine months

but that was only the beginning.

I carry you still—in my thoughts,

in my prayers, in every breath I take

when you're not near.

You are my forever ache

the sweet pain of love

that never goes away.

I carried you in blood,

but now I carry you in spirit.

In dreams where I hold you again,

in fears I silence for your sake.

You will never outgrow me.

Not in the places that matter.

Because I am your first home

and you, my eternal heartbeat.

The Man I Had to Become

When I first heard I'd be a father,

something broke open in me.

Fear and joy collided

in a moment that demanded

I rise.

I didn't know how,

but I knew I had to.

Not just to provide,

but to be present.

Not just to teach,

but to listen.

Not just to protect,

but to become a shelter.

Fatherhood didn't make me perfect

it made me real.

And each time my child looked at me

like I held the stars,

I remembered—

I don't have to be everything.

I just have to be there.

Present. Willing.

Growing with them, day by day.

The Secret Weight of Motherhood

They see the smiles,

the birthday cakes,

the matching outfits.

They don't see

the panic in the midnight hour.

The guilt.

The wondering if I'm enough.

The prayers whispered

into baby monitors

and school pickup lines.

Motherhood is beautiful—but heavy.

Not because our children are a burden,

but because our love for them

has no ceiling.

We break ourselves

so they never have to.

We sacrifice

without ever asking for thanks.

But we carry it—all of it

because to be their mother

is to wear a crown

no one else sees.

To My Child I Haven't Met Yet

Somewhere in the silence,

you exist.

Maybe only in my dreams.

Maybe waiting

to be placed in my arms

by time or by miracle.

But I already love you.

Already talk to God about you

like He's holding you close

until He sends you to me.

Maybe I'll birth you.

Maybe I'll meet you through adoption,

or another path I can't yet see.

But know this— you are wanted.

You are named

in the deepest part of me.

And when we meet,

I'll recognize you.

Not by face, but by spirit.

Because I've loved you

long before you ever called me

Mom or Dad.

Fatherhood Is Forgiveness

I thought I had to be flawless

never cry, never break, never fall short.

But fatherhood

showed me the power

of beginning again.

I've made mistakes.

Said the wrong things.

Worked too much.

Missed too many moments.

But love, real love, forgives.

Each time my child runs to me

even after I mess up

I learn grace again.

They don't need me perfect.

They need me present.

And humble enough

to say, "I'm sorry,"

and strong enough

to mean it.

Fatherhood isn't about pride.

It's about presence.

And the courage to keep becoming better.

Songs of the Womb

The womb is more than a place—
it is a prayer. A promise.
A beginning wrapped in darkness,
sung into existence
by a mother's faith and a father's hope.
It is where life takes shape
in the silence.
Where God forms miracles in secret.
And though the world forgets
what began there, the soul remembers.
There is music in the womb—
heartbeat lullabies, divine rhythms,
sacred songs passed down
in blood and bond.
To create, to carry, to protect
these are not small things.
They are the echoes
of God's own love.
And every child—no matter how they come
carries that song.
Forever.

Section V: Midnight Conversations

Theme: Late-night thoughts, spiritual wrestling, private prayer, divine dialogue.

Section V: Midnight Conversations will be a quiet and vulnerable journey into those sacred, restless hours—when the world sleeps, but the soul is wide awake. These poems will capture intimate reflections, silent battles, late-night prayers, regrets, hopes, and the unspoken dialogues we have with ourselves, with others, and with God beneath the moonlight

Psalm 63:6–7 (KJV)

"When I remember thee upon my bed and meditate on thee in the night watches. Because thou hast been my help, therefore in the shadow of thy wings will I rejoice.

Lamentations 2:19 (KJV)

"Arise, cry out in the night... pour out thine heart like water before the face of the Lord."

When the World Goes Quiet

It's not the sun that reveals the truth

it's the silence after midnight.

When the world goes quiet,

the noise inside gets loud.

There, in the hush,

I hear the weight of everything I carry.

Dreams I buried. Words I never said.

Questions I'm too afraid to ask.

I think about who I am when no one's looking.

The version of me that cries in the dark

but smiles in the morning. Sometimes I talk to God.

Not with fancy prayers, but with broken whispers.

"Am I enough?" "Why does it still hurt?"

"Can You really hear me?" And somehow,

even when heaven doesn't speak back,

peace answers. Not with thunder— but with stillness.

Maybe the quiet isn't empty.

Maybe it's full of things waiting to be heard.

Prayers with No Language

Sometimes, I can't find the words.

My heart is heavy,

but my mouth stays closed.

All I have is breath.

A sigh, a tear, a silent ache

throbbing in the middle of the night.

And yet— I know He hears.

Because prayer isn't always sentences.

Sometimes it's the way my body curls up in exhaustion,

the way I stare at the ceiling wondering if I'm seen.

It's the groan that escapes

when I think no one is listening.

But God hears groans.

He reads between the silence.

He understands pain

even when it speaks no language.

So I offer Him my stillness.

My breaking. My breath.

And He answers with peace.

Conversations I Never Had

I talk to ghosts.
Not the kind that haunt rooms
the kind that haunt choices.
The father I never understood.
The friend I pushed away.
The version of me that never got to be.
At night, they sit at the foot of my bed,
unseen but heavy.
I say things I should've said years ago.
"Why did you leave?"
"I forgive you." "I miss who I was
before the world made me hard."
Midnight becomes a confession booth
for the heart.
And every unspoken word finally finds air.
I know they can't answer.
But sometimes, just saying it
sets me free.

The Clock Doesn't Care

It's 2:47 AM and the clock ticks on

like it doesn't know I'm unraveling.

Time is cruel that way—moving forward

whether or not your heart does.

I stare at it,

wishing I could turn it back.

To moments I rushed through.

To words I didn't say.

To a version of me

that didn't ache so much.

But the clock doesn't care.

It ticks, and I breathe.

It ticks, and I remember.

It ticks, and I try again.

Maybe it's not supposed to care.

Maybe time is just the backdrop

and healing

is the real act of courage.

Nights I Sleep Next to My Fears

Some nights,

my fears crawl into bed with me.

They don't knock

they just slip under the covers

like they belong there.

"What if I fail?"

"Will they leave me?"

"Did I waste my life?"

I turn my back, but they stay.

Breathing down my neck

like memories I can't forget.

But I've learned

not to fight them anymore.

I just let them stay

let them speak.

Because when I name them,

they shrink.

And sometimes,

The most powerful thing I can do

is sleep beside my fears

and still wake up

braver.

A Letter to My Future Self

I hope you're not tired.

I hope you found the rest

we kept chasing.

I hope you're not bitter

that you forgave them

and forgave yourself too.

I hope you held onto joy,

even when grief made a home in you.

I hope you still believe

in love, in miracles, in second chances.

I hope you took the risks

I was too afraid to.

I hope you're proud of me

not because I was perfect,

but because I never gave up

when it would've been easier to quit.

I hope we meet someday

and you can say,

"You made it."

When Love Doesn't Come Back

Some nights,

I still hope you'll call.

I know you won't—

but hope doesn't always

need a reason.

You left, but love didn't.

It stayed, like an echo

that refuses to fade.

I talk to you in the silence.

I tell you what you missed—

how I'm learning to smile again,

how I've stopped checking

every notification like it's you.

But I still miss you.

Not just the way you loved me—

but the way I loved when I was with you.

Maybe you're gone for good.

Maybe that love was just a lesson.

But even so—

I'm grateful it lived, even if it died.

The Things I Can't Tell Them

They ask how I'm doing, and I smile.

"Good," I say. "Just tired."

But they don't know

the weight I carry

when the sun goes down.

They don't know

I cry in the shower,

pray in the car,

and sometimes stare at walls

longer than I should.

They don't know

how often I question my worth,

my purpose, my place.

But I keep going not because it's easy,

but because quitting isn't an option

when people depend on your strength.

So I say I'm okay,

and I fight silently.

Because some battles are too sacred to explain.

Midnight Is When I Remember

Midnight is memory's hour.

Not 10, not 11—

but when the world is still enough

for the past to rise like mist.

I remember people I didn't get to keep.

The version of me

before pain etched lines in my smile.

I remember joy

how it felt to laugh without heaviness.

And sometimes,

I let those memories wash over me

without resistance.

Not because I want to go back

but because they remind me I lived.

And if I lived once,

I can live again.

Conversations with God at 3AM

I don't come with a polished prayer.

Just a tired heart

and trembling hands.

I talk to God

like He's sitting on the edge of my bed,

like He already knows

but still wants to hear me say it.

"I'm tired."

"I don't know what to do."

"Please don't give up on me."

And He listens.

Even when I ramble.

Even when I doubt.

Even when I fall asleep

mid-prayer.

He doesn't need eloquence.

He just wants honesty.

So I bring Him my brokenness

night after night and somehow,

I leave whole.

Section VI: The Weight of Mercy

Theme: Forgiveness, grace, undeserved favor, compassion, redemption.

Section VI: The Weight of Mercy will delve into the soul's wrestling with grace, guilt, redemption, and divine compassion. These poems will explore what it means to be forgiven, to forgive, to carry the heaviness of past sins, and to finally let mercy wash over it all.

Micah 7:18–19 (KJV)

"Who is a God like unto thee, that pardoneth iniquity... he will turn again, he will have compassion upon us; he will subdue our iniquities..."

Titus 3:5 (KJV)

"Not by works of righteousness which we have done, but according to his mercy he saved us..."

The Weight of Mercy

It is not light— this thing called mercy.

It does not float like feathers or fall

like soft rain. It is heavy

because it bears

what I was never strong enough to carry.

It looks at my sins without flinching.

It walks into my shame

and refuses to turn away.

I spent years trying to earn

what was always meant to be given.

I fasted, I prayed, I wept—

but mercy was already there, waiting.

It doesn't erase the past,

but it rewrites the ending.

It tells the broken, "You are still worthy."

It tells the guilty, "You are still loved."

It tells the unworthy, "I never left."

So I carry this mercy now— not because I deserve it,

but because I was chosen to be redeemed.

And even if I fall again,

mercy will not fail to catch me.

Grace Wore My Scars

I tried to hide them

the cuts, the bruises,

the wounds that time couldn't erase.

But grace came gently

and didn't ask me to explain.

It rolled up its sleeves,

and wore my scars like armor.

It didn't say, "You should be better by now."

It said, "I see it all, and I still choose you."

In a world that loves perfection,

grace found beauty in my flaws.

I don't know why.

But I know how it feels

to be touched without judgment,

held without condition.

Grace wore my scars until I learned

to love them myself.

Mercy Met Me in the Mud

I didn't find mercy in a cathedral

or a choir's echo.

I found it in the mud.

When I had nothing to offer

but broken promises

and trembling hands.

I had fallen again, failed again,

lied to myself again.

But mercy didn't ask me to clean up first.

It knelt beside me, lifted my chin,

and called me "beloved."

Not "sinner." Not "shameful." Not "lost cause."

Just "beloved."

That's when I knew— mercy doesn't live

in perfect places.

It dwells in the dirt

and redeems what others discard.

The Man I Used to Be

Sometimes I hear his voice—

the man I used to be.

The one who hurt people

because he was hurting.

He was proud but empty.

Strong but scared.

Hard but hollow.

He shows up sometimes

in memories and regrets,

in old habits I haven't fully buried.

But I don't hate him anymore.

I understand him. And I've forgiven him.

Because God did.

Mercy isn't just about moving forward.

It's about turning around

and saying to your old self,

"You don't define me anymore."

The Guilt That Tried to Own Me

It whispered, night after night

"You are not enough."

"You'll never be clean."

"Look at what you've done."

Guilt is not loud.

It's relentless.

It plants seeds

and waters them in the dark.

But I learned

that guilt doesn't get the final say.

Not when grace enters the room.

Grace doesn't argue with guilt.

It simply shines.

And shadows don't win

when light shows up.

I still hear guilt sometimes.

But now, I know how to answer:

"I've been forgiven.

Go whisper somewhere else."

I Don't Deserve This Kind of Love

It doesn't make sense.

How He keeps chasing me

when I keep running.

How He calls me

when I stop listening.

How He blesses me

when I keep breaking

everything He gives me.

I've known human love

it leaves when it's tired.

It withdraws when you fail.

It puts limits on grace.

But not His love.

His love waits at the door.

Leaves the ninety-nine.

Sits beside the sinner

without shame.

And every time I say,

"I don't deserve this,"

He answers,

"That was never the point."

When Forgiveness Found Me

I wasn't looking for it.

I thought I had to earn it—

prove I was sorry enough,

clean enough, holy enough.

But forgiveness doesn't knock.

It walks through locked doors.

It sees the mess and sits down anyway.

I was still in the middle of my sin

when it came.

No altar. No choir.

Just a whisper inside:

"You are still Mine."

That's when I knew—

forgiveness finds us

when we least expect it and need it most.

Ashes and Altars

I burned everything down—

my peace, my pride, my purpose.

And in the ashes, I built an altar.

Not with gold or perfection,

but with pain

and prayers that cracked like glass.

And still, He showed up.

Not to scold me, but to sit with me.

Not to shame me, but to remind me:

"I can make beauty from ashes."

So I gave Him my ruins.

And He gave me resurrection.

The Quiet After Repentance

No lightning. No applause. Just quiet.

The kind of quiet

that settles after you pour it all out—

the guilt, the excuses, the pretending.

it's not a dramatic moment. It's a sigh.

A soft exhale of the soul.

You say, "I'm sorry.

And you mean it.

And somehow, in that stillness,

you feel held.

That's the grace of God

it doesn't always roar.

Sometimes, it simply stays.

I Am Not Who I Was

I wear the same skin,

but my soul is different.

I used to live

in survival mode

grabbing what I could,

hiding what hurt.

But mercy changed my posture.

It made me stand up straighter.

Speak softer.

Love deeper.

I still have scars

but they are proof of healing.

I still remember the darkness

but I don't fear it anymore.

Because now I walk

with light in my bones

and forgiveness in my lungs.

I am not who I was.

And by grace,

I never will be again.

Section VII: When the Spirit Sings

Theme: Spiritual freedom, divine presence, worship, holy healing, union with God.

Section VII: When the Spirit Sings is the final movement of Cries from the Deep, a place of sacred uplift where the soul, after passing through fire, pain, love, and mercy, begins to rise. These poems will echo themes of spiritual awakening, divine intimacy, holy surrender, and the unshakable presence of God through everything.

Zephaniah 3:17 (KJV)

"The Lord thy God in the midst of thee is mighty; he will save, he will rejoice over thee with joy; he will rest in his love, he will joy over thee with singing."

John 4:24 (KJV)

"God is a Spirit: and they that worship him must worship him in spirit and in truth."

When the Spirit Sings

It doesn't need a microphone or a pulpit.

The Spirit sings

in the hush between heartbeats,

in the tears you cry

when no one else is watching.

It sings in sighs too deep for words,

and in laughter

that comes after long suffering.

I have heard it— not with ears,

but with something inside me

that remembers Heaven.

It sang when I was empty.

It hummed when I was full.

It wept with me,

then turned those weeps into worship.

No band. No choir. Just presence.

Holy. Unseen. Undeniable.

And when the Spirit sings

your soul will know the melody.

Because it was written in you

before you were ever born.

Breath of the Divine

I felt it before I saw it—
a stirring in my chest,
a warmth in my bones.
Not wind. Not fire. Something deeper.
It was the breath of the Divine,
moving through my spirit
like wind through wheat.
No scripture in hand, no preacher near
just me and a whisper that said,
"I am here." In that moment,
I wasn't lost. I wasn't broken.
I was His. And sometimes
That's all the healing we need
to remember we are still His.

Heaven Touched Earth in Me

It didn't happen in a temple.

It didn't happen in a thunderclap.

It happened on a Tuesday morning,

while washing dishes,

with tired eyes and a heart worn thin.

And suddenly,

Heaven touched Earth inside of me.

It wasn't loud. It wasn't grand.

It was peace where there had only been panic.

It was rest

where there had only been racing thoughts.

That's how God comes sometimes—

quiet enough to miss

if you're not listening,

powerful enough to change everything

if you are.

Surrender in the Silence

There were no words left. Only silence.

And in that silence, I let go.

I let go of needing to be strong.

I let go of the fight.

I let go of trying to earn

what was already given.

And in surrender, I didn't fall apart.

I found God.

He didn't come to punish.

He came to pour. Not wrath

but oil. Not fire— but peace.

And I knew,

as the silence deepened

This was worship.

Not with hands lifted,

but with nothing held back.

My Spirit Remembers

Even when I forget,

my spirit remembers.

The sound of Eden's breeze.

The voice that called light into being.

It knows the rhythm of redemption.

It knows the name above all names.

This body may tire.

This mind may doubt.

But the spirit within me

never forgets its home.

That's why I still sing

when I'm broken.

Why I still pray

when I don't understand.

Because some part of me

was made

for glory.

The Holy That Lives in Me

I thought holiness

was found in buildings,

in rituals, in robes.

But I found it

in tears on a bathroom floor,

in kindness I didn't deserve,

in the courage to try again.

The Holy lives in me.

It walks with me

into every room, every mistake,

every miracle. Not to condemn,

but to remind me:

"I chose you. I dwell in you.

You are mine."

That truth changes how I breathe.

Spirit Over Flesh

Flesh says fight. Spirit says forgive.

Flesh says hide. Spirit says heal.

I've followed the flesh

and it left me starving.

I've obeyed the Spirit— and I found life.

It's not always easy.

The war is daily.

But each time I choose Spirit,

I taste eternity.

And the more I walk with Him,

the more my feet move toward peace.

Because in this battle, surrender is victory.

The Sound of Deliverance

It's not always loud.

Sometimes, deliverance

sounds like a deep breath

you haven't been able to take for years.

It sounds like chains falling

in a quiet heart.

Like laughter

after long sorrow.

It sounds like your own voice

saying, "I forgive them."

Or maybe,

"I forgive me."

Deliverance isn't just escaping.

It's awakening.

It's standing where you once fell.

It's walking where you once crawled.

And when the sound comes—

You'll know it.

Because it won't just shake the room.

It will shake your soul free.

I Am His Vessel

I am not my shame.

I am not my past.

I am not the voices

that tried to define me.

I am His vessel.

Formed in fire.

Poured from pain.

But still whole.

Still chosen.

He didn't ask for perfection

He asked for surrender.

And I gave Him

what little I had.

Now I carry His oil.

Now I speak His name.

And though I've been cracked,

I leak light

everywhere I go.

When the Spirit Sings

It begins with stillness.

A breath. A tremble.

A hush before the holy.

Then it rises—

not from the lips, but from the soul.

The Spirit sings.

Not in language, but in light.

Not in melody, but in mercy.

It sings through my scars.

Through my story.

Through every time I broke

and He made something

beautiful anyway.

It sings when I sleep.

It sings when I weep.

It sings when I think I've lost Him—

just to remind me He never left.

And when the Spirit sings,

the darkness listens. The heart opens.

The soul comes home.

And I— I become a song.

Section I: Beneath the Silence

Reflection: This section gives voice to the quiet struggles, the kind that hide behind smiles, strength, and silence. It explores the inner worlds we don't often share: the weight of loneliness, the pain of being unseen, and the courage it takes to keep going. These poems speak to the battles fought in private, offering comfort to anyone who has ever whispered "I'm fine" when they were anything but.

Psalm 34:18 (NIV)

"The Lord is near to the brokenhearted and saves the crushed in spirit."

Section II: Shattered Mirrors

Reflection: In this section, we confront the distorted images we've carried of ourselves. Shattered mirrors symbolize how trauma, failure, and shame can cloud our self-worth. But these poems also offer the hope that through grace, healing, and truth, we can reclaim our reflection and see ourselves with love.

1 Corinthians 13:12 (NIV)

"For Now we see only a reflection as in a mirror; then we shall see face to face."

Section III: Dust and Water

Reflection: These poems examine the essence of our humanity—how fragile we are, yet how divine our origins. We are made of dust, shaped by water, held together by spirit. This section reminds us that even in brokenness, there is beauty, and in imperfection, a divine signature.

Genesis 2:7 (NIV)

"Then the Lord God formed man of the dust of the ground and breathed into his nostrils the breath of life; and man became a living being."

Section IV: Songs of the Womb

Reflection: This section sings of origin, creation, and the sacred bond between parent and child. From the first flutter of life to the deep call of fatherhood, these poems honor the voices and stories carried in the womb. It celebrates motherhood, fatherhood, and the legacies we pass on.

Jeremiah 1:5 (NIV)

"Before I formed you in the womb I knew you, before you were born I set you apart."

Section V: Midnight Conversations

Reflection: These poems are for the nights when sleep escapes us, and the soul begins to speak. They reflect spiritual yearning, honest prayers, and quiet revelations that only the darkness can draw out. Here, we meet God not in perfection—but in vulnerability.

Psalm 16:7–8 (NIV)

"Even at night my heart instructs me... I keep my eyes always on the Lord."

Section VI: The Weight of Mercy

Reflection: This section is drenched in grace. It carries the story of being pursued by mercy—even when we feel unworthy. The poems speak of forgiveness, redemption, and the healing that comes when we finally accept, we are still loved.

Psalm 23:6 (NIV)

"Surely goodness and mercy shall follow me all the days of my life, and I shall dwell in the house of the Lord forever."

Section VII: When the Spirit Sings

Reflection: In the final section, the soul lifts its voice in praise. These poems are pure communion—moments where heaven touches earth. Whether whispered or shouted, the spirit's song rises out of sorrow, shaped by fire and redeemed by faith. This is where brokenness becomes worship.

1 Chronicles 16:23 (NIV)

"Sing to the Lord, all the earth; proclaim his salvation day after day."

Final Benediction

"When the Deep Breaks Open"

Now that you've journeyed through the depths—

Through womb and wound, silence and shadow,

Let this be your blessing:

May your tears become rivers of healing.

May your past become the soil for your purpose.

May your silence become a sacred song.

And may your spirit rise, even from the lowest place.

Go forth in boldness,

Covered in mercy,

Guided by whispers,

And strengthened by every scar you refused to let define you.

You are not broken. You are becoming.

You are not alone. You are anointed.

And from this day forward, may your soul never again shrink

For fear of being too much.

You were made for the deep.

Now rise with the Spirit—and sing.

Amen.

www.ingramcontent.com/pod-product-compliance
Lightning Source LLC
Chambersburg PA
CBHW071204160426
43196CB00011B/2193